Medical Korean for

영어 화자를 위한
병원 한국어

장미영(Mi-yeong Jang)·김철수(Cheol-soo Kim)

English Speakers

역락

영어 화자를 위한 병원 한국어

Medical Korean for English Speakers

초판1쇄 인쇄 2014년 3월 2일 | **초판1쇄 발행** 2014년 3월 10일
지은이 장미영 · 김철수
펴낸이 이대현 | **편집** 이소희
펴낸곳 도서출판 역락 | **등록** 제303-2002-000014호(등록일 1999년 4월 19일)
주소 서울시 서초구 동광로 46길 6-6 문창빌딩 2층
전화 02-3409-2058(영업부), 2060(편집부) | **FAX** 02-3409-2059 | **이메일** youkrack@hanmail.net
ISBN 979-11-85530-16-1 93700

정가 18,000원

재물을 잃으면 조금 잃는 것이다. 명예를 잃으면 많은 것을 잃는 것이고, 건강을 잃으면 모든 것을 잃는 것이다. 건강이 없으면 행복도 없다. 건강은 인생의 핵심이자 의욕의 자극제다. 그래서 건강만큼 중요한 것은 세상에 없다고 한다.

몸이 아프면 세상이 지옥 같지만, 나으면 세상은 지상낙원으로 변한다. 갑자기 아프거나 돌발 사고를 당했을 때, 보살펴 줄 사람을 찾지 못한다면 크게 서러울 것이다. 그런데 보살펴 줄 사람이 있는데도 그 사람에게 자신의 아픈 상태를 제대로 말하지 못해서 적절한 도움을 받지 못한다면 그것처럼 답답한 일도 없다.

외국에 나가면 날씨도 다르고 물도 다르고 음식도 다르고 잠자리도 달라진다. 게다가 외국인들은 낯선 땅에 낯선 사람과 있다는 것 자체에 긴장한다. 타국에서 생활한다는 것은 타국이라는 것만으로도 정신적 압박이 되는 것이다.

15년 넘게 외국인을 가르치면서, 자기 몸의 상태를 그 나라 사람에게 알기 쉽게 설명할 수 있는 교육이 필요하다는 것을 절실히 느꼈다. 어떤 증세가 언제부터 나타났는지, 통증이 어느 정도인지, 어떤 부분이 어떻게 아픈지, 어떻게 도와주기를 원하는지를 표현할 수 있어야 한다. 그와 더불어 도움을 주는 사람들이 묻는 말도 이해할 수 있어야 한다. 특히 병원을 어떻게 이용하는지, 병원에서는 주로 어떻게 말하고 어떻게 이해하는지를 알면 무척 유용할 것이다.

필자는 그간 외국인들에게 한국어와 한국문화를 교육해 왔다. 그런데 정작 정규수업 시간보다 수업 시간 외에 외국인들과 보내는 시간이 더 많았다. 교통사고를 당했다거나, 축구를 하다가 다리가 부러졌다거나, 농구를 하다가 손이 삐었다거나, 목욕탕에서 미끄러져 걸을 수 없다거나, 생리통이 심하다거나, 귀걸이 때문에 귀가 찢어졌다거나, 온몸에 두드러기가 났다거나, 배가 심하게 아프다거나, 귀에 파리가 들어갔다거나, 계단에서 굴러 떨어졌다는 전화에 밤낮을 가리지 않고 약국과 병원을 찾아야 했다. 어떤 때는 한국의 민간요법까지 동원해가면서, 통증을 호소하는 외국인 곁을 밤새 지켜야 했다. 위급했던 상황을 돌이켜 생각하면 지금도 등골이 오싹하다.

이 책은 병원에서 유용하게 사용할 수 있는 한국어 표현들로 구성되었다. 책의 구성은 병원에서 사용하는 서류 작성법, 병원을 이용하는 법, 아픈 증상을 표현하는 법, 응급실을 이용하는 법, 내과, 이비인후과, 비뇨기과, 안과, 피부과, 치과, 성형외과, 산부인과 이용하는 법, 병명, 의사와 환자 사이의 대화에서 주로 사용하는 표현, 약과 관련된 표현, 체질과 관련된 표현, 한국 음식 이름 순으로 되어 있다.

여러 가지 경험과 오랜 궁리 끝에 책의 내용이 채워졌다. 결정적으로는 필자에게 아픔을 호소했던 외국인들 덕분에 이 책이 나오게 된 것 같다. 병원에 관한 필자의 질문에 성실히 답변해 주었던 전주 예수병원 이비인후과 이시영 의사 선생님의 도움도 컸다.

네 명의 아이들을 낳아 기르면서 필자가 겪었던 여러 가지 사고 경험도 이 책을 쓰는 데 보탬이 되었다. 세 명의 아이를 연달아 유산했던 일, 유산 후유증으로 몸의 반쪽이 마비되었던 일, 네 명의 아이를 집에서 출산하면서 겪었던 일, 출산 후유증으로 온갖 통증에 시달렸던 일, 벽에 걸어 놓은 시계가 떨어져 잠자던 아이를 덮쳤던 일, 문틈에 아이의 손가락이 낀 줄 모르고 방문을 닫았던 일, 아이의 목에 생선가시가 박혔던 일, 뜨거운 냄비를 의자 삼아 앉았던 아이가 엉덩이에 화상을 입었던 일…… 회상만으로도 경험했던 당시의 고통이 떠올라 눈물이 앞을 가린다.

　필자의 뜻에 공감하고 선뜻 영어 번역을 맡아주신 전주대학교 김철수 교수님께 깊은 감사를 드린다. 영어 원어민 교수님들이 들려 준, 영어 강사로서 또는 유학생으로서 한국에서 겪은 다양한 경험담 또한 필자에게 큰 도움이 되었다. 이 책의 출판을 흔쾌하게 수락해 주신 역락출판사 이대현 대표께도 감사를 전하고 싶다.

2014년 새봄

천잠산 자락의 전주대 연구실에서

문학박사 장미영

Losing money is losing a little, loosing honor is losing much, and losing health is losing everything. There is no happiness without health. Health is the core of life and a trigger of enthusiasm. That's why it is said nothing is more important than health in the world.

To a sick person the world is like a hell, but to a healthy person it changes into a paradise. We will feel sorrowful if we have no one to help us when we get sick and have an emergent accident. However, we feel much more sorrowful if we have a person to help us but we cannot explain our situation correctly, failing to get a proper assistance.

When you go overseas, everything changes, including climate, water, food and sleeping places. Further, foreigners get nervous just because they live with strangers in a strange land. Such a life gives them unendurable stress.

Having taught Korean to foreigners for 15 years I have felt it urgent to teach foreigners how to express their physical state. It is necessary for the foreigners to be able to explain where and how much it hurts and how they want to be helped. Also they have to be able to understand the questions of the helpers. Especially the information about how to use a hospital and specific usages in the hospital will be of great use for them.

I have taught foreigners Korean language and culture. However, I have spent more time with foreigners in extra hours than in class hours. Most of the time I had to help them find out a pharmacy and a hospital as they called and complained that they had a traffic accident, had the leg broken after a soccer play, or sprained the wrist after basketball play. Some of them couldn't walk after slipping down on the bathroom, some had severe rashes in the body, some had a severe stomachache, some had a fly in the ear, and even some fell on the stairs.

Sometimes I had to stay up at night sitting next to a foreigner complaining pains and taking care of them with folk remedies. The recollection of such times of danger freezes my blood.

This book contains diverse Korean expressions useable in Korean hospitals, including the ways to fill out the documents, use hospitals, express the symptoms, and to use the medical departments such as internal medicine, ENT, urology, ophthalmology, dermatology, dental clinic, plastic surgery, and OB/GYN. It also contains the names of diseases, some useful expressions between a doctor and a patient, some terminologies concerning medicine, physical constitution, and the names of Korean food.

This book is a culmination of diverse experiences and deliberation. Conclusively, I owe the publication of this book to the foreigners who complained their pain to me. I am also in great debt in the help of Dr. Lee Shi-young in the ENT clinic of Jesus Hospital in Jeonju, who sincerely answered my questions about a hospital.

Plenty of accidents I experienced in bringing up my four kids are also of great help for me. Among the experiences are three miscarriages, paralysis due to the miscarriages, giving birth to four kids, and lots of pain after the childbirth. One day a clock fell on one of my kids sleeping in the room, another kid had a fish bone stuck in his throat, and the other burned his buttocks after sitting on a hot pot. All the memories remind me of my tearful pain in those times.

I extend my gratitude to professor Cheol-soo Kim at Jeonju University, who gladly agreed to join this project as an English translator in sympathy with my intention. The experiences of the native speaker professors, who have lived in Korea as language teachers and overseas students, have also been great help to my work. The publication of this book has been facilitated by the support of the director of Youkrack Publishing Company, which is gratefully acknowledged.

In the march of 2014,

from an office of Jeonju University at the bottom of Mt. Cheonjam

Mi-young Jang, Ph. D.

　1990년대 후반 중국을 비롯한 아시아 대륙에서 시작된 '한류'의 열풍이후, 결혼과 취업 등의 정착된 목적뿐 아니라 관광과 사업 등 일시적인 목적으로 이미 우리의 이웃이 되어 있거나, 또는 다가오고 있는 외국인들을 통해 우리나라는 이미 세계화의 중심으로 부상하고 있다고 해도 과언이 아닐 것이다.

　이처럼 우리 안에 이미 구현되어있는 다문화성은 우리로 하여금 새로운 책임 의식을 느끼게 한다. 그것은 곧 우리의 도움과 관심을 바라며 우리나라를 찾는 사람들에게 그들이 원하는 바를 자유로이 소통할 수 있도록 우리의 마음과 눈과 귀를 열어 그들의 소리를 들어주고, 또 우리의 입을 열어 그들이 듣고자 하는 말을 전해주는 것이다.

　그중 가장 절실한 것은 인간의 가장 원초적인 문제, 즉 의식주와 의료적 필요에 따른 의사소통의 기회를 열어주는 것이라 할 수 있을 것인데, 바로 이러한 시기에 외국인 화자들을 위한 책자 발간을 준비한 장미영 교수의 의도는 참으로 시의적절한 일이라 아니할 수 없다.

　이미 중국어와 일본어 화자를 위한 병원용어집을 편찬한 장 교수가 영어 화자를 위한 동일한 책자를 구상하고 본인에게 영문번역으로 동참할 것을 권면했을 때, 한편으로는 미묘한 흥분이, 또 다른 한편으로는 다소간의 두려움이 엄습함을 느꼈다. 그 흥분은 30년 이상 영어를 공부하고 가르쳐온 사람으로서, 나의 짧은 지식과 경험이 누군가에게 큰 도움이 될 수 있을 것이라는 기대감에서 왔을 것이고, 그 두려움은 과연 그 풍부한 우리말의 의미들이 정확하게 전달되어서 이것을 필요로 하는 사람들에게 진정한 도움이 될 수 있을 것인가 하는 의구심에서 기인되었을 것이다.

개인적으로, 전공으로 공부한 영문학과 영국에서의 유학생활 그리고 십여 년간 섬겨온 교회의 영어 예배부에서의 경험을 통해 여러 가지 방법으로 외국인들을 소소히 도와 온 경험은 있으나 이와 같은 본격적인 작업에 참여해 본 적은 없는 본인으로서도 이 기회는 매우 아름답고도 의미 있는 인생의 경력이 될 것이라고 확신한다. 다행히 주한 미 8군 의무 사령부에서 근무한 본인의 경험이 의료 용어를 영어로 옮기는 데 다소나마 도움이 될 것이라는 얄팍한 자신감으로 이 위대한 작업에 참여할 수 있게 됨을 감사하게 생각한다.

오랜 경험과 궁리 그리고 다양한 상담의 과정을 통해서 구체화된 장 교수의 불인지심의 결과로 꼼꼼하고 상세하게 정리해 놓은 각종 의료 상황을 영어로 옮기는 과정에서 우리말 특유의 뉘앙스를 영어로 옮기는 데 있어서 적지 않은 어려움이 있었던 것이 사실이다. 예컨대, 공식적인 병명이나 증상 또는 치료의 절차 등의 번역은 그 자체의 대응어들의 존재로 인하여 그닥 큰 문제가 없었으나, 환자가 자신의 증상을 설명하면서 사용하게 되는 다양한 형용사와 부사의 표현들은 영어로 옮기는데 많은 고민을 야기하였다.

한편으로 이 책자는 "영어 화자를 위한 병원한국어"라는 제목을 갖고 있지만, 다른 한편으로는 우리말의 다양하고 풍부한 증상 표현을 외국인들에게 알려줄 수 있는 "한국인을 위한 의료영어"로서의 성격도 함께 지니고 있다고 자부한다. 더욱이 제20과에서 다루고 있는 음식의 종류와 이름, 재료 및 조리법 등에 대한 내용은 한국의 음식이 지니고 있는 고유의 풍미를 상세히 설명함으로써, 우리의 음식문화를 상세히 세계에 알릴 수 있는 기회를 제공할 것이라고 생각한다.

미국인 영어교사의 감수를 받아 표현의 정확성에 만전을 기하고자 최대한의 노력을 기울였으나, 그럼에도 불구하고 발견될 수 있는 오류는 순전히

본 번역자의 책임일 것이며, 그러한 오류들은 추후 지속적이고 면밀한 검토를 통해 수정해 갈 것이다.

모쪼록 이 책이 영어화자와 외국어 화자 간의 의사소통 상의 오해를 극소화 하고 더 나아가서 양 문화권의 원활하고 폭넓은 교제에 일조하기를 소원하며, 끝으로 이 의미 있는 작업에 불비한 번역자의 참여를 허락하고, 이런 저런 이유로 번역작업의 완성을 차일피일 미루어온 번역자의 게으름을 너그러이 용납하고 인내해 준 장미영 교수에게 깊은 감사를 표한다.

2014년 새봄
전주대학교 스타센터 연구실에서
문학박사 김철수

Since the strong craze of "Korean Wave" in the late 1990s starting from Asian countries including China, plenty of foreigners have come to Korea for the stable purposes of marriage and jobs and transient purposes of tourism and business. It is not too much to say that Korea has already become the center of globalization owing to the people, who have become or becoming our neighbor.

Such multiculturalism, which has embedded in our lives, urges us to have a new sense of responsibility. That is, we have to be able to open our eyes and ears to see and listen to the words of those who come to our country expecting our help and care, and open our mouth to transmit what they want to hear to them.

The utmost is to offer them an opportunity to communicate the most basic problems such as clothing, food, housing and medical necessity. In such a period of time, the intention of professor Mi-yeong Jang, who prepared a medical handbook for English speaker, is sure to be a timely reaction.

When professor Jang, who has published the medical handbooks for the speakers of Chinese and Japanese, encouraged me to join her new project for the English speakers as a translator, I had both delicate excitement and not a little fear. The excitement may have come from the expectation that, as a person having lived with English for over 30 years, my trivial knowledge and experience might be of any help for someone, and the fear from the doubt if my work might be properly used to transmit the affluent meanings of Korean language to those who need them in clear and correct English.

Personally, I have helped some foreigners in trifles through my experiences in the study of English literature as my major, in the United Kingdom as a overseas graduate student, and in my church as a coordinator of English worship service, but I have never participated in such a well-organized helping project. Thus I come to be sure that this will be a very beautiful and significant experience in my life career. Fortunately and gratefully enough, I can be confident that I will be able to get some help in translating the Korean medical terms into English thanks to my military experience as a medic at the 18th Medical Command of the 8th United States Force in Korea.

It is true that I have had not a little difficulty in translating diverse medical situations, which professor Jang has arranged with much elaboration and minuteness as a result of her spirit of compassion concretized through long experience, consideration and diverse counselling, according to the specific nuance of Korean language. For instance, the translation of the official names and symptoms of diseases and the steps of the treatment was not so difficult owing to the corresponding expressions. However, the expressions with adjectives and adverbs which the patients use in subjectively expressing their symptoms has caused some agony.

One the one hand, this book is entitled as "Medical Korean for English Speakers," however, on the other hand, it can surely function as "Medical English for Korean Speakers," with which Korean people will be able to communicate diverse and affluent expressions of symptoms in English. Especially the contents about the kinds, names, material and recipe of Korean food will provide an opportunity to spread the Korean food culture to the world by explaining its innate flavor and taste in detail.

As a translator, I have exerted myself to eliminate the possibility of errors in expressions and meanings, which nevertheless might be found in close readings. I clearly claim that all the responsibilities are on the translator himself and that I, as a translator, will continue to revise them through subsequent close reading.

Hopefully, this book will be of a little service to minimize the misunderstanding in the communication between the speakers of English and Korean, and finally, I would like to extend my gratitude to professor Jang, who has allowed me to participate in such a meaningful project as this and showed generous patience to the laziness of the translater, having detained the completion of this significant work.

March 2014

From my office in the Star Center, Jeonju University

Cheol-soo Kim, Ph. D.

목차 Contents

I. 접수할 때

Registration

01 기본 병원 용어
Basic Hospital Terminology

1. 시설에 관한 용어 Terms for Facilities

1) 병원 Hospital [*Byeongwon*]

2) 의원 Clinic [*Euiwon*]

3) 병동 Ward [*Byeongdong*]

4) 대기실 Waiting Room [*Daegishil*]

5) 수술실 Operation Room [*Susulshil*]

6) 마취실 Aesthesia Room [*Machwishil*]

7) 입원실 Sick Room [*Ibwonshil*]

8) 중환자실 Intensive Care Unit(ICU) [*Junghwanjashil*]

9) 엑스레이실 X-ray Room [*Ex-rayshil*]

10) 검사실 Laboratory [*Geomsashil*]

11) 사무실 Office [*Samushil*]

12) 원장실 Director's Office [*Wonjangshil*]

13) 부원장실 Vice-director's Office [*Buwonjangshil*]

14) 수납 창구 Reception/Payment Desk [*Sunapchanggu*]

15) 의사실 Doctor's Office [*Euisashil*]

16) 간호사실 Nurses' Station [*Ganhosashil*]

17) 식당 Cafeteria [*Sikdang*]

18) 취사실 Kitchen [*Chwisashil*]

19) 신생아실 Nursery [*Shinsaengashil*]

20) 수유실 Lactation Room [*Suyushil*]

21) 창고 Storage [*Changgo*]

2. 호칭에 관한 용어 Titles

1) 의사 선생님 Doctor [*Euisa Seonsaengnim*]

2) 간호사 선생님 Nurse [*Ganhosa Seonsaengnim*]

3) 환자 Patient [*Hwanja*]

4) 보호자 Guardian [*Bohoja*]

5) 간병인 Care Worker [*Ganbyengin*]

6) 호스피스 Hospice Volunteer [*Hospice*]

7) 문병객 Visitor [*Munbyeonggaek*]

8) 방문객 Visitor [*Bangmungaek*]

9) 낯선 사람 Stranger [*Notseon Saram*]

10) 모르는 사람 The person you don't know [*Morunun Saram*]

3. 의료 관련 용어 Medical Terminology

1) ① 접수 Registration [*Jeopsu*]

② 접수처 Registration Desk [*Jeopsucheo*]

2) ① 수납 Payment [*Sunap*]

② 수납처 Payment Desk [*Sunapcheo*]

③ 원무과 Hospital Administration [*Wonmugwa*]

3) 예약 Appointment [*Yeyak*]

① 시간 예약 Appointment of Time [*Shigan Yeyak*]

② 담당 의사 예약 Appointment with the Doctor [*Damdang Euisa Yeyak*]

4) 검진 Examination [*Geomjin*]

① 정기 검진 Periodic Examination [*Jeonggi Geomjin*]

② 건강 검진 Physical Examination [*Geongang Geomjin*]

③ 건강검진기록부 Physical Examination Record [*Geongang Geomjin Girokbu*]

④ 진료 기록 카드 Medical Treatment Card [*Jillyo Girok Card*]

5) ① 진찰 Consultation [*Jinchal*]

② 진찰실 Consultation Room(Doctor's Office) [*Jinchalshil*]

③ 진찰비 Consultation Fee(Doctor's Bill) [*Jinchalbi*]

6) 검사 Tests [*Geomsa*]

① 소변 검사 Urine Test [*Sobyeon Geomsa*]

② 대변 검사 Stool Test [*Daebyeon Geomsa*]

③ 혈액 검사 Blood Test [*Hyeolaek Geomsa*]

④ 심전도 검사 ECG(Electrocardiogram) Test [*Shimjeondo Geomsa*]

⑤ 암 검사 Cancer Test [*Am Geomsa*]

⑥ 조직 검사 Biopsy [*Jojik Geomsa*]

⑦ 내시경 검사 Endoscopy [*Naeshigyeong Geomsa*]

⑧ 검사비 Test Fee [*Geomsabi*]

6) ① 의료보험 Medical Insurance [*Euiryo Boheom*]

② 의료보험증 Medical Insurance Card [*Euiryo Boheomjeung*]

③ 의료보험료 Medical Insurance Fee [*Euiryo Boheomnyo*]

7) ① 진찰권 Consultation Ticket [*Jinchalgwon*]

② 진찰일 Consultation Date [*Jinchalil*]

③ 진찰비 Consultation Fee (Doctor's Bill) [*Jinchalbi*]

④ 진찰실 Consultation Room (Doctor's Office) [*Jinchalshil*]

8) ① 외래 의사 Extern [*Waerae Euisa*]

② 외래 환자 Outpatient [*Waerae Hwanja*]

9) ① 초진 First Consultation [*Chojin*]

② 재진 Second Consultation [*Jaejin*]

③ 재검진 Re-examination [*Jaegeomjin*]

④ 검진비 Examination Fee [*Geomjinbi*]

10) ① 진료 Medical Treatment [*Jillyo*]

② 진료 기록 Treatment Record [*Jillyo Girok*]

③ 진료기록부 Treatment Record Card [*Jillyo Girokbu*]

④ 진료비 Treatment Fee [*Jillyobi*]

⑤ 진료실 Treatment Room [*Jillyoshil*]

⑥ 무료 진료 Free Medical Treatment [*Muryo Jillyo*]

⑦ 외래 Outpatient [*Waerae*]

⑧ 병동 Ward [*Byeongdong*]

⑨ 입원 Hospitalization [*Ibwon*]

⑩ 퇴원 Discharge from Hospital [*Twaewon*]

⑪ 양식 Forms [*Yangshik*]

⑫ 진단서 Diagnosis Record [*Jindanseo*]

⑬ 소견서 Clinical Record [*Sogyeonseo*]

⑭ 동의서 Written Consent [*Dongeuiseo*]

11) 증상 Symptom [*Jeungsang*]

① 경상 Slight Injury [*Gyeongsang*]

② 중상 Serious Injury [*Jungsang*]

③ 중증 Serious Symptom [*Jungjeung*]

12) ① 치료 Treatment [*Chiryo*]

② 입원 치료 Hospital Treatment [*Ibwon Chiryo*]

③ 방문 치료 Homecare [*Bangmoon Chiryo*]

④ 약물 치료 Drug Treatment [*Yakmul Chiryo*]

⑤ 물리 치료 Physical Therapy [*Muli Chiryo*]

⑥ 치료비 Medical Bills, Doctor's Bill [*Chiryobi*]

13) ① 마취 Anesthesia [*Machwi*]

② 전신 마취 General Anesthetic [*Jeonshin Machwi*]

③ 부분 마취 Partial Anesthetic [*Bubun Machwi*]

④ 국소 마취 Local Anesthetic [*Gukso Machwi*]

14) ① 수술 Operation, Surgery [*Susul*]

② 대수술 Complicated Operation [*Daesusul*]

③ 큰 수술 Big Operation [*Keun Susul*]

④ 간단한 수술 Simple Operation [*Gandanhan Susul*]

⑤ 수술비 Operation Charges [*Susulbi*]

15) ① 입원 Hospitalization [*Ibwon*]

② 입원 수속 Hospitalization (Admission) Procedures [*Ibwon susok*]

③ 퇴원 Discharge [*Twaewon*]

④ 퇴원 수속 Discharge Procedures [*Twaewon Susok*]

⑤ 입원비 Hospital Bill [*Ibwonbi*]

16) ① 면회 시간 Visiting Hours [*Myeonhwae Shigan*]

② 면회 수칙 Visiting Regulations [*Myeonhwae Suchik*]

17) ① 처방 Prescription [*Cheobang*]

② 처방전 Prescription Slip [*Cheobangjeon*]

18) ① 진단 Diagnosis [*Jindan*]

② 진단서 Diagnosis Record [*Jindanseo*]

19) ① 건강보험 Health Insurance [*Geongang Boheom*]

② 암보험 Cancer Insurance [*Am Boheom*]

③ 생명보험 Life Insurance [*Saengmyeong Boheom*]

④ 상해보험 Accidental Insurance [*Sanghae Boheom*]

20) ① 모자 수첩 Mother-and-child Handbook [*Moja Suchop*]

② 아기 앨범 Baby Album [*Agi Album*]

21) 구급상자 First-Aid Kit [*Gugeup Sangja*]

① 소독약 Antiseptic [*Sodongyak*]

② 반창고 Bend-Aid [*Banchanggo*]

③ 솜 Cotton swabs [*Som*]

④ 거즈 Gauze [*Gauze*]

⑤ 붕대 Bandage [*Bungdae*]

⑥ 해열제 Fever Remedy, Anti-Febrile Medication [*Haeyeolje*]

⑦ 소화제 Digester; Peptic. [*Sohwaje*]

⑧ 진통제 Pain-killer [*Jintongje*]

⑨ 연고 Ointment [*Yeongo*]

⑩ 체온계 Body Thermometer [*Cheongye*]

⑪ 마스크 Gauze Face Mask [*Mask*]

⑫ 인대 Eyepatch, Eye Bandage [*Andae*]

⑬ 탈지면 Surgical Cotton [*Taljimyeon*]

⑭ 핀셋 Tweezers [*Pincet*]

⑮ 족집게 Tweezers [*Jokjipgae*]

22) ① 전화 Telephone / Contacts [*Jeonhwa*]

② 비상 전화 Emergency Call [*Bisang Jeonhwa*]

③ 긴급 전화 Urgent Call [*Gingeup Jeonhwa*]

23) 기타 Others

① 구급차 Ambulance [*Gugeupcha*]

② 화재 Fire [*Hwajae*]

③ 경찰 Police [*Gyeongchal*]

④ 교통사고 Traffic Accident [*Gyotong Sago*]

⑤ 날씨 Weather [*Nalssi*]

4. 진료 과목

1) 내과 Internal Medicine Department [*Naegwa*]

2) 순환기 내과 Internal Medicine for Circulatory organs [*Sunhwangi Naegwa*]

3) 호흡기 내과 Internal Medicine for Respiratory organs [*Hoheupgi Naegwa*]

4) 소화기 내과 Internal Medicine for Digestive organs [*Sohwagi Naegwa*]

5) 내분비 내과 Internal Medicine for Internal Secretion [*Naebunbi Naegwa*]

6) 외과 Surgical Department [*Waegwa*]

7) 흉부외과 Chest Surgery Department [*Hyungbu Waegwa*]

8) 신경외과 Neurosurgery Department [*Shinkyung Waegwa*]

9) 정형외과 Orthopedics Department [*Jeonghyeong Waegwa*]

10) 성형외과 Plastic Surgery Department [*Seonghyeong Waegwa*]

11) 산부인과 OB-GYN Department [*Sanbuingwa*]

12) 비뇨기과 Urology Department [*Binyogigwa*]

13) 소아과 Pediatrics Department [*Soagwa*]

14) 피부과 Dermatology Department [*Pibugwa*]

15) 정신과 Psychiatry Department [*Jeongshingwa*]

16) 한방과 Oriental Medicine Department [*Hanbanggwa*]

17) 안과 Ophthalmology Department [*Angwa*]

18) 치과 Dental Department [*Chigwa*]

19) 이비인후과 Ear, Nose, and Throat(ENT) Department [*Eebeenhugwa*]

20) 가정의학과 Home-doctoring Department [*Gajeong Euihakgwa*]

21) 재활의학과 Rehabilitation Medicine Department [*Jaehwal Euihakgwa*]

22) 영상의학과 Radiology Department [*Yeongsang Euihakgwa*]

02 개인 및 가족 의료 정보
Individual and Family Medical Information

1. 핵심어 Key Words

① 이름(한자, 영문) Name (Chinese, English)

② 성별 Sex

③ 국적 Nationality

④ 여권 번호 Passport Number

⑤ 외국인등록번호 Alien Registration Number

⑥ 주민등록번호 ID Number

⑦ ㉠ 생일 Birthday

   ㉡ 생년월일 Date and Year of Birth

⑧ 나이 Age

⑨ 연락처 Personal Contact

   ㉠ 집 전화 Home Phone Number

   ㉡ 직장 전화 Office Phone Number

   ㉢ 전자 메일 E-mail Address

⑩ 입국 일자 Date of Entrance

⑪ 주소 Address

2. 단어 Words

1) 남편(아내) Husband(Wife)

① 남편(아내) 이름 Husband's (Wife's) Name

② 남편(아내) 생년월일 Husband's (Wife's) Birthday

③ 남편(아내) 연락처 Husband's (Wife's) Personal Contact Information

㉮ 남편(아내) 직장 전화 Husband's (Wife's) Office Phone Number

㉯ 남편(아내) 핸드폰 Husband's (Wife's) Mobile Phone Number

④ 남편(아내) 병력 Husband's (Wife's) Medical History

2) 응급 시 연락 번호 Emergency Contacts

3) 신체 Body Shape

① 키 Height

② ㉠ 체중 Weight

㉡ 몸무게 Weight of the Body

㉢ 임신 전 체중 Weight before Pregnancy

㉣ 현재 체중 Present Weight

4) 혈액형 Blood Type

① 본인 혈액형 Patient's Blood Type

② 배우자 혈액형 Spouse's Blood Type

③ 아들 혈액형 Son's Blood Type

④ 딸 혈액형 Daughter's Blood Type

5) 과거 병력 Past Medical History

① 고혈압 High Blood Pressure/ Hypertension

② 당뇨 Diabetes

③ 결핵 Tuberculosis (TB)

④ 간염 Hepatitis

⑤ 암 Cancer

ㄱ 간암 Liver Cancer ㄴ 유방암 Breast Cancer

ㄷ 위암 Stomach Cancer ㄹ 자궁암 Womb Cancer

ㅁ 폐암 Lung Cancer ㅂ 피부암 Skin Cancer

ㅅ 식도암 Esophageal Cancer ㅇ 난소암 Ovarian Cancer

ㅈ 대장암 Colon Cancer ㅊ 갑상선암 Thyroid Cancer

ㅋ 방광암 Cystic Cancer ㅌ 골수암 Bone Cancer

ㅍ 소장암 Small Intestine Cancer ㅎ 희귀암 Rare Cancer

⑥ 갑상선 Thyroiditis

⑦ 외상 Trauma

⑧ 천식 Asthma

⑨ 심장질환 Cardiac Disorder

⑩ 기타 Other Diseases

3. 유용한 표현 Useful Expressions

1) 신장 Height

   ① 신장이 몇이에요? What's your height?

   ② 키가 몇이에요? How tall are you?

   ③ 161cm[백육십일]이에요. I'm 161 centimeters tall.

2) 체중 Weight

   ① 체중이 몇이에요? What's your weight?

   ② 몸무게가 몇이에요? How heavy are you?

   ③ 50kg[오십 킬로]예요. 50 kilograms

3) 혈압 Blood Pressure

   ① 혈압이 몇이에요? What's your blood pressure?

   ② 120/80[백이십에 팔십]이에요. One hundred and twenty over eighty (120/80).

   ③ ㉠ 고혈압이에요? Do you have high blood pressure [hypertension]?

      ㉠ 네, 고혈압이에요. Yes. I have high blood pressure. [hypertension]

   ④ ㉠ 저혈압이에요? Do you have low blood pressure [hypotension]?

      ㉡ 네, 저혈압이에요. Yes. I have low blood pressure [hypotension].

   ⑤ ㉠ 혈압이 정상이에요? Do you have normal blood pressure?

      ㉡ 네, 정상이에요. Yes. I do.

4. 현장 한국어 Korean in Practice

1) 어디가 아프세요? Where does it hurt?

   ① 어떤 증상으로 오셨나요? What are your symptoms?

   ② 목구멍이 아파서 왔어요. I have a sore throat.

   ③ 언제부터 그런 증상이 나타났나요? When did it start?

   ④ 3일 전부터 아프기 시작했어요. It started three days ago.

   ⑤ 어느 부분이 제일 아픈가요? Where does it hurt most?

   ⑥ 여기요. Here.(Right here!)

2) 전에 입원한 적이 있나요? Have you ever been hospitalized?

   ① 전에 입원한 적이 있어요. I have been hospitalized before.

   ② 전에 입원한 적이 없어요. I have never been hospitalized.

3) 전에 수술 받은 적이 있나요? Have you ever had an operation?

   ① 전에 수술 받은 적이 있어요. I have had an operation.

   ② 전에 수술 받은 적이 없어요. I have never had an operation.

4) 계속 먹고 있는 약이 있나요? Are you on medication?

   ① 계속 먹고 있는 약이 있어요. Yes, I'm on medication.

   ② 계속 먹고 있는 약이 없어요. No, I'm not on medication.

5) 시력이 얼마예요? What's your eyesight?

   ① ㉠ 좌측 시력이 얼마예요? What's your left eyesight?

   ㉡ 1.0[일 점 영]이에요. It's one point zero.

▶ 노안 (Presbyopic)
40대 후반 이후에 찾아
오는 퇴행성 시력감퇴 현
상으로, 일정한 크기 이
상의 글씨가 잘 보이지
않아 돋보기를 필요로 하
게 된다.
Presbyopic is a degenera-
tive failing of eyesight
one may experienc e
after one's forties. The
people with presbyopic
require reading glasses
to read very small letters.

② ㉠ 우측 시력이 얼마예요? What's your right eyesight?

㉡ 0.8[영 점 팔]이에요. It's zero point eight.

㉢ ㉠ 눈, 좋아요? Do you have good eyesight?

㉡ 좋아요. 양쪽 다 1.5[일 점 오]예요. Yes. Both eyes are one point five.

㉢ 눈, 나빠요. I have bad eyesight.

㉣ 안경 안 쓰면 안보여요. I can't see without my glasses.

㉤ 교정시력은 좋아요. My corrected eyesight is good.

㉥ 난시예요. I have a bad astigmatism.

㉦ 노안이에요. I am presbyopic.

6) 청력이 좋아요? Do you have good hearing?

㉠ 좌측 청력은 좋아요. I have good hearing in my left ear.

㉡ 왼쪽은 잘 들려요. I can hear well with my left ear.

㉢ 우측 청력은 안 좋아요. I have bad hearing in my right ear.

㉣ 오른쪽은 잘 안 들려요. I can't hear well with my right ear.

7) 간단한 질문을 할게요. Let me ask you some brief questions.

① 어떤 일을 하시나요? What do you do for a living?

② 커피는 하루에 몇 잔 마시나요? How much coffee do you drink a day?

③ 담배를 피우세요? Do you smoke?

④ 술을 자주 마시나요? Do you drink alcoholic beverages often?

⑤ 현재 임신 중인가요? Are you pregnant?

⑥ 마취 부작용이 생긴 적 있나요? Have you had any side effects

with anesthesia?

8) 처방해 드릴게요. Let me give you a prescription.

   ① 처방된 약은 아프지 않더라도 꼭 드세요.

     You should take the prescribed medicine even when you are not sick.

   ② 수술 후 2일 동안 얼음찜질 해주세요.

     Please apply an ice pack for 2 days after operation.

   ③ 수술 후 3일 동안 힘든 일하지 마세요.

     Please avoid hard work for three days after the operation.

   ④ 수술 후 1주일 동안 운동하지 마세요.

     Please don't exercise for a week after the operation.

   ⑤ 목욕을 오래하지 마세요. Please don't take a long bath.

   ⑥ 몸을 따뜻하게 하시기 바랍니다. Please keep yourself warm.

   ⑦ 땀을 많이 흘리는 일을 피하세요. Please avoid too much sweating.

9) 제가 담당 의사입니다. I'm the doctor in charge.

   ① 수술하기로 결정하셨어요? Have you decided to have the operation?

   ② 수술 동의서를 써 주세요. Please fill out the written consent.

   ③ 한국 내에 연락 가능한 주소와 전화번호를 써 주세요.

     Please write down your Korean address and phone number where you can be contacted.

10) 제가 환자예요. I'm the patient.

   ① 치료할 때 많이 아파요? Does the treatment hurt very much?

   ② 상담은 끝났어요? Is the consultation over?

③ 보험으로 해결되나요? Can it be covered with my insurance?

④ 임신 중에도 치료 받을 수 있어요?

　　Is it safe to undergo the treatment while I'm pregnant?

⑤ 마취하면 안 아파요? Isn't it painful to be under anesthesia?

⑥ 한 번 시술하면 언제까지 효과가 있어요?

　　How long will the treatment continue to produce positive effects?

⑦ 치료는 언제 끝나요? When will the treatment be over?

⑧ 치료 기간이 얼마나 걸려요? How long will the treatment take?

03 아픈 증상
Symptoms

1. 핵심어 Key Words

1) 몸 Body

2) 열 Fever

3) 한기 Chills, Cold

4) 땀 Sweat

5) 부기 Swelling

6) 몸무게 Weight

7) 통증 Pain (Ache)

8) 오한 Chills

9) 복통 Stomachache

10) 두통 Headache

11) 흉통 Chest Pain

12) 구토 Vomit

13) 감기 Cold

14) 가려움 Itching

15) 화끈거림 Feeling Hot

16) 수포 Blister

17) 두드러기 Rash

18) 점 Birthmark

19) 화상 Burn

20) 변비 Constipation

21) 알레르기 Allergy

2. 단어 Words

1) 여기 HERE

① 여기가 아파요. It hurts here.

② 이쪽이 아파요. I have pain on this side.

2) 몸 BODY

① 몸이 안 좋아요. I don't feel well.

② 몸이 피곤해요. I'm tired.

③ 온 몸이 아파요. I'm stiff and sore.

④ 몸이 무거워요. I'm feeling sluggish.

⑤ 몸이 거뜬해요. I feel fine.

⑥ 몸이 가벼워요. I feel like flying.

3) 열 FEVER

① 열이 나요. I have a fever

② 열이 많아요. I have a high fever.

③ 열이 높아요. My body temperature is high.

④ 열을 식혀요. Please cool down the fever.

⑤ 열을 내려요. We need to reduce the fever.

⑥ 열을 재 봐요. Please check the body temperature.

⑦ 체온을 재 봐요. Why don't you check the body temperature?

⑧ 체온 잴 게요. Let me check your temperature.

⑨ ㉠ 체온이 얼마예요? What's my temperature?

　　㉡ 38℃[삼십팔도]예요. It's thirty-eight degrees Celsius.

4) 한기 CHILL, COLD

① 한기가 들어요. I'm feeling chilly.

② 몸이 추워요. I feel cold.

③ 몸이 오슬오슬 추워요. I have shivering chills.

④ 몸이 떨려요. I'm chilly.

⑤ 오한이 나요. I'm having chills.

5) 땀 SWEAT

① 땀이 나요. I am sweating.

② 땀이 많이 나요. I am sweating too much.

③ 식은땀이 나요. I have night sweats.

④ 밤에 잘 때 땀이 많이 나요. I sweat heavily at night.

⑤ 손바닥에서 땀이 많이 나요. I sweat a lot from my palm.

⑥ ㉠ 땀이 많아요. I sweat a lot.

　㉡ 땀이 적어요. I scarcely sweat.

　㉢ 땀이 안 나요. I don't sweat.

　㉣ 땀이 없어요. I have no sweat.

　㉤ 아무리 더워도 땀 한 방울 안 흘려요.

　　I don't sweat even in the hottest weather.

6) 부기 SWELLING

① 얼굴에 부기가 있어요. My face is swollen.

② 얼굴이 부었어요. My face is puffy.

③ 부기가 빠졌어요. The swelling has gone down.

④ 부기가 없어졌어요. The swelling is gone.

⑤ 부으면 안 좋아요. It's not a good sign if you are swelling.

7) 몸무게 WEIGHT

① 몸무게가 얼마예요? How much do you weigh?

② 몸무게가 늘었어요. I've put on some weight.

③ 몸무게가 줄었어요. I've lost some weight.

④ 몸무게를 늘리고 싶어요. I'd like to put on some weight.

⑤ 몸무게를 줄이고 싶어요. I'd like to lose some weight.

⑥ 살 찌고 싶어요. I want to gain weight.

⑦ 살 빼고 싶어요. I want to lose some weight.

3. 유용한 표현 Useful Expressions

1) 통증을 어떻게 말해요? How can I express my pain?

   ① 어디가 아파요? Where does it hurt?

      ㉠ 밥만 먹으면 배가 아파요. I have stomachaches right after meals.

      ㉡ 여기가 아파요. I have a pain here.

      ㉢ 이쪽이 아파요. This part hurts.

      ㉣ 그쪽이 아파요. That part hurts.

      ㉤ 거기가 아파요. I have a pain right there.

      ㉥ 그 위쪽으로 아파요. The pain is in the upper part.

      ㉦ 그 아래쪽으로 아파요. I have pain down there.

      ㉧ 오른쪽 옆구리 밑이 아파요. My right side hurts.

      ㉨ 왼쪽 옆구리 밑이 아파요. My left side hurts.

   ② 머리 HEAD

      ㉠ ㉮ 머리가 아파요. I have a headache.

        ㉯ 머리가 매우 아파요. I'm getting a very bad headache.

      ㉡ 머리가 지끈지끈 아파요. I have a pounding headache.

      ㉢ ㉮ 머리가 무거워요. My head feels heavy.

        ㉯ 머리가 띵해요. I have a dull headache.

        ㉰ 머리가 빙빙 돌아요. I feel dizzy.

      ㉣ 머리가 쪼개질 듯이 아파요. I have a splitting headache.

      ㉤ 머리가 깨질 듯이 아파요. I have an awful crashing headache.

      ㉥ 머리가 터질 듯이 아파요. My head is pounding.

      ㉦ 머리가 갈라질 듯이 아파요. My head is splitting.

ⓗ 머리가 조금 아파요. I have a little headache.

ⓩ 머리가 약간 아파요. I have a slight headache.

ⓒ 머리가 매우 아파요. I have a bad headache.

ⓚ ㉮ 머리가 울려요. My head is pounding.

    ㉯ 골이 흔들려요. My brain is pounding.

    ㉰ 열이 있어요. I have a fever.

ⓣ 뒷골이 당겨요. The back of my neck is stiff.

ⓟ 머리가 계속 아파요. I have continuous headaches.

ⓗ 편두통이 있어요. I have migraines.

③ 눈 EYE

    ㉠ 눈이 아파요. My eyes hurt.

    ㉡ 눈알이 빠지게 아파요. My eyes are popping out with pain.

    ㉢ 눈물이 줄줄 흘러요. My tears are continuously coming out.

    ㉣ 눈이 잘 충혈 돼요. My eyes are often bloodshot.

    ㉤ 눈이 가려워요. My eyes itch.

    ㉥ 눈이 따가워요. My eyes feel irritated.

    ㉦ 눈꺼풀이 부었어요. My eyelids are swollen.

    ㉧ 물체가 두 개로 보여요. I have blurred vision.

    ㉨ 눈에 뭐가 들어갔어요. I have something in my eyes.

    ㉩ 눈병이 생겼어요. I have an eye disease.

    ㉪ 시력이 점점 나빠지고 있어요. My eyesight is getting worse.

④ 귀 EAR

    ㉠ 귀가 아파요. My ear hurts.

ⓛ 왼쪽 귀가 아파요. My left ear hurts.

ⓒ 오른쪽 귀가 아파요. My right ear hurts.

ⓡ 귀가 막힌 것 같아요. My ears feel plugged up.

ⓜ 귀가 멍멍해요. I feel as if I got deafened.

ⓗ 귀가 울려요. My ear rings.

ⓢ 귀에서 분비물이 나와요. There is some discharge from my ear.

ⓞ 귀가 잘 안 들리고 어지러워요. I can't hear well and feel dizzy.

ⓩ 귀가 잘 안 들려요. I can't hear well.

ⓒ 귀속으로 벌레가 들어갔어요. I have a bug in my ear.

ⓚ 귀에서 냄새가 나요. Something smells bad in my ear.

ⓣ 귀에서 진물이 나요. There is a watery discharge from my ear.

ⓟ 귀에서 소리가 나요. I hear a buzzing in my ear.

ⓗ 이명 때문에 괴로워요. I can't stand the tinnitus in my ear.

⑤ 코 NOSE

ⓖ 코가 막혔어요. I have a stuffy nose.

ⓛ 코가 자주 막혀요. I have nasal congestion.

ⓒ 코가 항상 막혀 있어요. My nose is always stopped up.

ⓡ 코피가 자주 나요. I often have nosebleed.

ⓜ 콧물이 나와요. I have a runny nose.

ⓗ 코에서 고름이 나와요. Pus is oozing out of my nose.

ⓢ 재채기를 자주 해요. I sneeze a lot.

ⓞ 코 속이 간지러워요. My nose itches inside.

ⓩ 먼지 알레르기가 있어요. I'm allergic to dust.

ⓒ 꽃가루 알레르기가 있어요. I have hay fever.

ㅋ 코맹맹이 소리를 해요. I speak in a nasally voice.

⑥-1 목 THROAT

ㄱ 목구멍이 너무 아파요. My throat hurts very much.

ㄴ 목이 쓰라려요. I have a sore throat.

ㄷ 침도 못 삼켜요. I can't swallow my spit because of the pain in my throat.

ㄹ 침 삼킬 때 목이 아파요. My throat hurts when I swallow my spit.

ㅁ 음식을 삼킬 때 목이 아파요. My throat hurts when I swallow food.

ㅂ 목구멍이 부은 것 같아요. My throat feels swollen.

ㅅ 편도선이 부었어요. My tonsils are swollen.

ㅇ 목안이 따끔따끔해요. My throat feels scratchy.

ㅈ 목이 쉬었어요. My voice is hoarse.

⑥-2 입 MOUTH

ㄱ 입 안이 써요. My mouth tastes bitter.

ㄴ 입이 말랐어요. My mouth is dry.

ㄷ 입안이 끈적거려요. My mouth is sticky.

ㄹ 입에서 단내가 나요. I feel something burning in my mouth.

ㅁ 입냄새가 심해요. My breath smells bad.

⑦ 이 TOOTH

ㄱ 이가 아파요. I have a toothache.

ⓛ 이가 심하게 아파요. I have a bad toothache.

ⓓ 위 어금니가 아파요. My upper molar hurts.

ⓡ 아래 송곳니가 아파요. My lower canine hurts.

ⓜ 사랑니가 나느라고 아파요.

I have a toothache because my wisdom teeth are growing.

ⓗ 충치가 있어요. I have a decayed tooth.

ⓢ 이가 부러졌어요. My tooth broke off.

ⓞ 이가 빠졌어요. My tooth was taken out.

ⓙ 치아가 고르지 못해요. My teeth have grown irregular.

ⓒ 치석이 있어요. I have plaque.

ⓚ 잇몸이 부었어요. My gums are swollen.

ⓣ 잇몸에서 피가 나요. My gums are bleeding.

ⓟ 틀니가 맞지 않아요. My dentures don't fit.

ⓗ 교합이 잘 안 맞네요. My teeth are a little misaligned.

⑧ 손 HAND

ⓖ 손이 저려요. My hand cramps.

ⓛ 손마디가 쑤셔요. My finger joints are stiff and sore.

ⓓ 손이 뜨거워요. My hands feel hot.

ⓡ 손이 시려요. My hands are freezing.

ⓜ 손목이 시큰거려요. I have a sharp pain in my wrist.

ⓗ 손가락을 베었어요. I cut my finger.

ⓢ 뜨거운 물에 손을 데었어요. I burned my hand on hot water.

ⓞ 손바닥에 가시가 박혔어요. I've got a splinter on my palm.

ⓙ 손바닥 껍질이 벗겨져요. I lost some skin on my palm.

ㅊ 손톱이 찢어졌어요. I chipped a nail.

ㅋ 손가락이 삐었어요. I sprained my finger.

ㅌ 손가락을 망치로 때렸어요. I struck my finger with a hammer.

ㅍ 둘째손가락이 문틈에 끼었어요. I shut my finger in a door.

ㅎ 손에 감각이 없어요. My hand has gone numb.

⑨ 발 FEET

ㄱ 발이 커요. I have big feet.

ㄴ 발이 작아요. I have small feet.

ㄷ 볼이 넓어요. My feet are wide.

ㄹ 볼이 좁아요. My feet are narrow.

ㅁ 엄지발가락이 밖으로 휘었어요. My big toe is bent to the outside.

ㅂ **무지 외반증**이에요. It's hallux valgus.

ㅅ 평발이에요. I am flat-footed.

ㅇ 새끼발가락이 퉁퉁 부었어요. My little toe is swollen.

ㅈ 새끼발가락 발톱이 쪼개졌어요.

   The toe nail on my little toe is chipped.

ㅊ 네 번째 발가락에 발톱 무좀이 생겼어요.

   My fourth toenail has fungal infection.

ㅋ ㉮ 발에 무좀이 생겼어요. I have athlete's foot.

   ㉯ 발에 무좀이 심해요. I have severe athlete's foot.

ㅌ 발뒤꿈치가 찌릿찌릿 아파요. There is a shooting pain in my heels.

ㅍ 발뒤꿈치 각질이 심해요. There are some dead skin cells on my heel.

▸ 무지 외반증
엄지 발가락이 바깥쪽으로 휘는 현상
Hallux valgus is a condition where the big toe is bent toward the outer side of the foot

ㅎ 발뒤꿈치 굳은살을 긁어냈어요. I removed callus from my heels.

⑩ 다리 LEG

ㄱ 다리가 아파요. I have a pain in my leg.

ㄴ 뒷다리가 당겨요. My leg muscles feel tight.

ㄷ 오른쪽 다리가 통증이 심해요. I have a terrible pain in my right leg.

ㄹ 다리가 저려요. I have a cramp in my leg.

ㅁ 다리에 쥐가 났어요. I've got a cramp in my leg.

ㅂ 다리 근육이 뭉쳤어요. My leg muscles are cramped up.

ㅅ 무릎이 굽혀지지 않아요. I can't bend my knee.

ㅇ 양쪽 무릎이 화끈거려요. I have a searing pain in my knees.

ㅈ 넓적다리가 아파요. I have a pain in my thigh.

ㅊ 다리가 골절 됐어요. I have a fracture in my leg.

ㅋ 다리가 부러졌어요. I broke my leg.

ㅌ 발목을 삐끗했어요. I twisted my ankle.

ㅍ 발목을 삐었어요. I sprained my ankle.

ㅎ 발목을 접질렸어요. I wrenched my ankle.

⑪ 배 STOMACH

ㄱ 식욕이 없어요. I have no appetite.

ㄴ 식욕이 좋아요. I have a good appetite.

ㄷ 식욕이 왕성해요. I have a big appetite.

ㄹ 밥을 잘 먹어요. I eat well.

ⓜ 밥을 잘 못 먹어요. I can't eat well.

ⓑ ㉮ 소화가 잘 안돼요. I have indigestion

ㄴ 헛배가 불러요. I have gas in my stomach.

ㄷ 배가 더부룩해요. I feel bloated.

ⓢ ㉮ 윗배가 아파요. I have a pain in the upper part of my belly.

ㄴ 아랫배가 아파요. I have a pain in the lower part of my belly.

ㄷ 옆구리가 아파요. I have a pain in my side.

ㄹ 옆구리가 움켜쥘 듯이 아파요. I have a twisting pain in my side.

ⓞ ㉮ 배가 살살 아파요. I have an irritating stomachache.

ㄴ 배가 콕콕 쑤셔요. I have a sharp pain in my stomach.

ⓩ 구역질이 나요. I'm vomiting.

ⓒ 자주 토해요. I throw up frequently.

ⓚ 토할 것 같아요. I have nausea.

ⓣ 배에 가스가 차요. I have lots of gas in my stomach.

⑫ 배설기관 EXCRETORY ORGAN

㉠ 설사를 해요. I have diarrhea.

㉡ 김치만 먹으면 설사를 해요. Whenever I eat *kimchi*, I get diarrhea.

㉢ 변비에요. I am constipated.

㉣ 변비가 있어요. I have constipation.

㉤ 삼일에 한 번씩 화장실에 가요.

I go to the restroom once in three days.

㉥ 항문에서 피가 나요. I have anal bleeding.

ⓢ 대변에 피가 섞여 나와요. There's blood in my stool.

ⓞ 속이 메슥거려요. I feel nauseated.

ⓩ 식중독에 걸렸어요. I've got food poisoning.

ⓒ 저는 단 것을 좋아해요. I like sweet things.

ⓚ 저는 기름진 음식을 좋아해요. I like fatty food.

ⓔ 저는 매운 음식이 좋아요. I like spicy food.

ⓟ 방귀를 자주 뀌어요. I fart a lot.

⑬ 소변 URINATION

㉠ 오줌 누기 힘들어요. I have a hard time urinating.

㉡ 오줌을 눌 수 없어요. I can't pee.

㉢ 하룻밤에도 오줌을 누려고 세 번이나 일어나요.

I get up three times at night to take a piss.

㉣ 하루에 소변을 이십 번 이상 봐요.

I pee more than 20 times a day.

㉤ 오줌 누고 나면, 뭔가 남은 것 같아요.

I usually feel uncomfortable after urinating.

㉥ 오줌에 피가 섞여 나와요.

There is blood in my urine.

㉦ 오줌에 돌이 섞여 나왔어요.

I have a piece of grit in the urine.

(There are crystals in my urine.)

㉧ 얼굴이 붓고 손이 부어요.

My face and hands are swollen.

㉨ 오줌 눌 때 아파요. I have pain during urination.

ⓩ 생식기가 가려워요. My genital area is itching.

ⓣ 무모증 때문에 고민이에요. I'm worried about hairlessness [atrichosis].

⑭ 뼈 BONES

ⓐ 목이 뻣뻣해요. My neck feels stiff.

ⓑ 접촉사고로 목을 다쳤어요.

My neck was hurt in a traffic accident.

ⓒ 목에 감각이 없어요. My neck is numb.

ⓓ 근육을 다쳤어요. I hurt my muscle.

ⓔ 허리가 아파요. I have a back pain.

ⓕ 의자를 들다가 허리를 삐끗했어요.

I strained my back in lifting a chair.

ⓖ 허리에서 '툭' 하는 소리가 났어요.

I heard a cracking sound coming from my back.

ⓗ 허리가 끊어질 듯이 아파요. I have a severe backache.

ⓩ 허리 디스크예요. I have a herniate lumbar disc.

ⓒ 어깨가 빠졌어요. My shoulder is dislocated.

ⓚ 어깨뼈 근처가 아파요. I feel stiff in the shoulders.

ⓣ 어깨가 굳었어요. My shoulders got tight.

ⓟ 오십견이에요. I have frozen shoulders.

⑮ 팔 ARM

ⓐ 팔이 부었어요. My arm is swollen.

ⓑ 팔이 부러졌어요. My arm is broken.

ⓒ 팔에 쥐가 났어요. I've got a cramp in my arm.

ⓓ 팔꿈치가 까졌어요. I skinned my elbow.

ⓔ 팔꿈치 관절에 물이 찼어요. I have water in the elbow joints.

ⓕ 팔에 멍이 들었어요. I've got a bruise on my arm.

ⓖ 팔이 올라가지 않아요. I can't lift my arms.

ⓗ 헛짚어 손목이 꼬였어요. I twisted my wrist falling down on my hands.

ⓘ 팔에 물집이 생겼어요. I have a blister in my arm.

ⓙ 팔에 아토피가 있어요. I have an atopic disease in my arm.

ⓚ 팔꿈치에 티눈이 생겼어요. I have a callus in my elbow.

ⓛ 팔이 너무 가려워요. My arm is very itchy.

ⓜ 팔이 돌아갔어요. My arm is dislocated.

3. 현장 한국어 Korean in Practice

1) 입을 벌리세요. Open your mouth.

① 자, '아'하고 입을 벌리세요. Open your mouth and say, "Ah."

② 입을 다무세요. Close your mouth.

③ 입을 헹구세요. Please, gargle your mouth.

2) 쑤셔요. It aches.

① 콕, 콕 쑤셔요. I have a sharp pain.

② 바늘로 찌르는 듯이 쑤셔요. I have a stinging pain.

③ 온 몸이 다 쑤셔요. My body aches all over.

3) 근질근질해요. It itches.

　① 벌레가 기어가는 듯이 근질근질해요.

　　It feels like something is crawling.

　② 참을 만하게 가려워요. It itches, but it is bearable.

　③ 참기 어렵게 가려워요. It itches unbearably.

4) 숨이 차요. I am short of breath.

　① 쉽게 숨이 차요. I get short of breath often.

　② 숨쉬기가 어려워요. I have difficulty breathing.

　③ 숨 쉬는 것이 힘들 정도예요. I have trouble even taking a breath.

　⑤ 숨을 헐떡거려요. I am gasping for breath.

5) 기침이 나요. I cough.

　① 기침이 계속 나요. I just keep coughing.

　② 기침이 계속 나고 열이 약간 있어요.

　　I have a continuous cough and slight fever.

6) 어디가 아파요? Where does it hurt?

　① 병명이 뭐예요? What kind of disease is it?

　② 왜 아파요? Why am I sick?

　③ 통증을 어떻게 말해요? How can I express my pain?

7) 수술이 필요해요? Do I need to get an operation?

　① 수술하나요? Am I going to have an operation?

② 수술해야 되나요? Do I have to have an operation?

8) 비용은 얼마나 드나요? How much does it cost?

① 얼마예요? How much is it?

② 다 합쳐서, 비용이 얼마예요? How much is it in total?

9) 여드름이 자꾸 나요. I have pimples frequently.

① 온 몸에 두드러기가 났어요. I have a rash all over my body.

② 등에 여드름이 많아요. I have lots of pimples on my back.

③ 팔에 붉은 반점이 생겼어요. Some red flecks appeared on my arm.

④ 습진이 심해요. I have a bad case of eczema.

⑤ 발진이 있어요. My skin broke out in a rash.

⑥ **아토피**성 피부염이 있어요. I have an atopic dermatitis.

⑦ 손에 물집이 생겼어요. I have a blister in my hand.

⑧ 코에 종기가 났어요. I have a boil on my nose.

⑨ 너무 가려워서 긁었어요. I scratched very hard because it was too itching.

▸ 아토피는 일종의 만성적 피부병으로 감염성이 없는 가려움증이다. Atopy is a type of eczema. It is an inflammatory chronically occurring, non—contagious, itchy skin disorder.

10) 생리가 없어졌어요. My periods stopped.

① 냉이 있어요. I have vaginal discharge.

② 대하가 있어요. I have leukorrhea.

③ 생리가 있다가 없다가 해요. My periods come and go.

④ 생리가 불규칙해요. My periods are irregular.

⑤ 생리 때가 아닌데 출혈이 있어요. I have untimely menstrual bleeding.

▸ 대하
대하는 여성의 생식기에 발생하는 백색 혹은 황색의 점액질의 분비물이다. Leukorrhea is thick, whitish or yellow vaginal discharge.

⑥ 생리를 일주일 넘게 해요. My period goes on over a week.

⑦ ㉮ 생리양이 많아요. I have heavy menstrual flow.

　㉯ 생리양이 적어요. I have light menstrual flow.

⑧ 생리불순이에요. I'm suffering from irregular menstruation.

⑨ 생리가 2주일 늦어요. My period is two weeks late.

⑩ 지난 달, 생리가 없었어요. I missed my period last month.

⑪ ㉮ 생리가 규칙적이에요. I have regular periods.

　㉯ 생리가 불규칙적이에요. I have irregular periods.

⑫ 지난 달 생리는 3일에 시작해서 10일에 끝났어요.

　My period started on the 3rd last month and finished on the 10th.

⑬ ㉮ 마지막 생리는 4월에 있었어요. My last period was in April.

　㉯ 최종월경은 4월에 있었어요. My last menstruation was in April.

병원 이용법
How to Navigate the Hospital

1. 핵심어 Key Words

1) 병원 Hospital

2) 접수 창구 Reception Desk

3) 보건소 Health Clinic

4) 약국 Pharmacy

5) 수납 Payment

6) 원무과 Administration

7) 간호사실 Care Worker

8) 간병인 Personal Nurse

9) 병동 Ward

10) 수술실 Operation Room

11) 마취 Anesthesia

12) 부작용 Side Effect

13) 전염 Contamination

14) 엑스레이(X-ray) Radiology

15) 링거 Intravenous(IV) Injection

16) 혈압 Blood Pressure

17) 컴퓨터 단층촬영 Computerized Tomography (CT)

18) **조영제**(造影劑) Contrast Agent

19) **금식** Fast

20) 체온 Body Temperature

21) 맥박 Pulse

22) 혈액 검사 Blood Test

2. 단어 Words

1) 신체 이름 Names of the Body Parts

① 얼굴 Face

② 머리 Head

③ 이마 Forehead

④ 눈썹 Eyebrow

⑤ ㉠ 눈 Eye

  ㉡ 코 Nose

  ㉢ 입 Mouth

  ㉣ 귀 Ear

⑥ ㉠ 손 Hand

  ㉡ 발 Foot

⑦ ㉠ 팔 Arm

  ㉡ 다리 Leg

⑧ ㉠ 살 Flesh

㉡ 뼈 Bone

⑨ ㉠ 팔목 Wrist

㉡ 발목 Ankle

⑩ ㉠ 팔꿈치 Elbow

㉡ 발꿈치 Heel

⑪ ㉠ 가슴 Chest

㉡ 배 Stomach

㉢ 등 Back

⑫ 생식기 Genitals

⑬ 배설기관 Excretory Organ

⑭ 항문 Anus

⑮ 피부 Skin

3) 병원이 뭐예요? What is a hospital[*Byeongwon*]?

① 병원은 몸이 아플 때 찾아가는 곳이에요.

You should go to a hospital when you are sick.

② 병원은 환자를 치료해주는 곳이에요.

A hospital is a place where patients are taken care of.

4) 병원의 종류에 대해서 알려 주세요. What kinds of hospitals are there?

(1) 병원은 크기에 따라

① 종합병원, ② 대학병원, ③ 전문병원, ④ 개인병원, ⑤ 보건소,
⑥ 보건지소 등이 있어요.

(1) Hospitals are categorized according to their size.

① a general hospital, ② a university hospital, ③ a specialized hospital, ④ a private hospital, ⑤ a health clinic, ⑥ a local branch of a health clinic.

(2) 전문 병원은 아픈 곳에 따라

① 안과, ② 소아과, ③ 정형외과, ④ 이비인후과, ⑤ 일반외과, ⑥ 산부인과, ⑦ 치과, ⑧ 신경외과, ⑨ 흉부외과, ⑩ 피부과, ⑪ 비뇨기과 등이 있어요.

(2) Specialized hospitals may have the following departments;

① Ophthalmology, ② Pediatrics, ③ Orthopedics, ④ Ear-nose-and-throat, ⑤ Surgery, ⑥ OB/GYN, ⑦ Dental medicine, ⑧ Neurosurgery, ⑨ Cardiothoracic surgery, ⑩ Dermatology, ⑪ Urology

㉮ 안과 : Department of Ophthalmology[*Angwa*]

㉠ 눈이 아플 때 안과에 가요.

If your eyes are sore, you should go to the ophthalmology department.

㉡ 시력이 나쁠 때 안과에 가요.

If you have bad eye sight, you should go to the ophthalmology department.

㉯ 소아과 : Department of Pediatrics[*Soagwa*]

㉠ 아기가 아플 때 소아과에 가요.

If your baby is sick, you should take him/her to the pediatrics department.

㉡ 어린이가 아플 때 소아과에 가요.

If your child is sick, you should take him/her to the pediatrics department.

ⓓ 정형외과 : Department of Orthopedics[*Jeonghyeong Waegwa*]

뼈를 다쳤을 때 정형외과에 가요.

When you injure a bone, you should go to the orthopedics department.

ⓔ 이비인후과 : Department of ENT (Ear-Nose-Throat)[*Eebeenhugwa*]

ㄱ 귀가 아플 때 이비인후과에 가요.

If you have an earache, you should go to the ENT department.

ㄴ 코가 아플 때 이비인후과에 가요.

If you have a problem with your nose, you should go to the ENT department.

ㄷ 목이 아플 때 이비인후과에 가요.

If you have a sore throat, you should go to the ENT department.

ㄹ 귀, 코, 목 등이 아플 때 이비인후과에 가요.

If you have a problem with your ear, nose and throat, you should go to the ENT department.

ⓕ 일반외과 : Department of General Surgery[*Ilbanwaegwa*]

몸의 상처를 치료할 때 외과에 가요.

You should go to the general surgery department if you have an injury in the body.

ⓖ 산부인과 : Department of OB/GYN[*Sanbuingwa*]

아기를 낳으려고 할 때 산부인과에 가요.

You should go to the OB/GYN department to give birth to a child.

(사) 치과 : Department of Dental Medicine[*Chigwa*]

이가 아플 때 치과에 가요.

You should go to the dental medicine department if you have a toothache.

(아) 신경외과 : Department of Neuro-surgery[*Shinkyungwaegwa*]

머리가 아프면 신경외과에 가요.

You should go to the neuro-surgery department if you have a severe headache.

(자) 흉부외과 : Department of Cardiothoracic surgery[*Hyungbuwaegwa*]

가슴이 아프면 흉부외과에 가요.

You should go to the cardiothoracic surgery department if you have a severe chest pain.

(차) 피부과 : Department of Dermatology[*Pibugwa*]

피부가 가려우면 피부과에 가요.

You should go to the dermatology department if you have a problem with your skin.

(카) 비뇨기과 : Department of Urology[*Binyogigwa*]

㉠ 생식기가 아프면 비뇨기과에 가요.

You should go to the urology department if you have problems with your genital organs.

ⓛ 배설기관이 아프면 비뇨기과에 가요.

You should go to the urology department if you have problems with your excretory organ.

3. 유용한 표현 Useful Expressions

1) 병원 접수창구는 어떻게 이용해요?

How do you use the reception desk in a hospital?

▶ 번호표
병원에서 진료를 받기
전에 번호표를 뽑아 순
서를 기다려야 한다.
Number slip : There are
ticket slips with numbers
on them, and you should
try and find one of those
before you go in the
waiting live.

① 병원에 들어가서 **번호표**를 뽑아요.

Enter the hospital and take a number slip.

② 번호를 부를 때까지 순서를 기다려요.

Wait until your number is called.

③ 자기 순서가 되면 접수창구에 의료보험증을 주세요.

When it is your turn, give your medical insurance card to the receptionist.

④ 그런 다음 창구 안내원의 안내에 따라 행동해요.

Then, follow the receptionist's direction.

⑤ 이름이나 번호를 부르면 진료실로 들어가요.

When your name or number is called, go into the doctor's office.

⑥ 진료가 끝나면 처방전을 받아요.

After you meet with the doctor, you will receive a prescription.

⑦ 접수창구에 가서 진료비를 내요.

Then, pay the receptionist a consultation fee.

2) 병원 접수창구 서류 Documents for the reception desk

① 환자 인적 사항 확인 Personal Identification of the Patient

환자 인적 사항(Personal Identification of the Patient)		
성명 Name	주민번호/외국인등록번호 Social Security Number Alien Registration Number	전화번호 Telephone Number
주소 Address	(우편번호 : Zip Code) 주소(Address) :	

② 내원 여부 확인 History of Treatment

최초 내원일 First Visit	년(Year) 월(Month) 일(Day)	
최종 내원일 Last Visit	년(Year) 월(Month) 일(Day)	
입원 여부 Previous Hopitalization Experience	있다/ Yes	없다/ No
	년 월 일부터 From _____	
	년 월 일까지 To _____	

③ 병원 방문 목적 확인 Purpose of Visit

병원 방문 목적 Purpose of Visit	
아파서 For Treatment	O
서류 떼러 For Document	

④ 진료과 접수 Registration for Treatment

진료과 Treating Departments				
정형외과 Orthopedics	신경외과 Neurosurgery	내과 Internal Medicine	치과 Dental Medicine	산부인과 OB/GYN
피부과 Dermatology	소아과 Pediatrics	안과 Ophthalmology	비뇨기과 Urology	이비인후과 ENT

3) 약국은 어떻게 이용해요? How do I use the pharmacy?

① 약국에 들어가서 순서를 기다려요.

Enter the pharmacy and wait for your turn.

② 자기 순서가 되면 병원에서 받은 처방전을 직원에게 주세요.

When it is your turn, give the prescription to the clerk.

③ 그런 다음 약사로부터 약을 받아요.

Receive your medicine from the pharmacist.

④ 약사의 설명을 잘 들으세요.

Listen carefully to the pharmacist's explanation.

⑤ 약값을 내요.

Pay for the medicine.

4) 의료보험 가입은 어떻게 해요?

How do I sig up for the Medical Insurance?

① 국민건강보험공단(1577-1000)에 문의해요.

You can call the National Health Insurance Corporation.(Toll-free phone 1577-1000)

② 영어 안내는 02-390-2000에 문의해요.

For English information, you can call 02-390-2000.

5) 초진이에요? Is this your first visit to this hospital?

6) 건강보험증 있어요? Do you have a Medical Insurance Card?

4. 현장 한국어 Korean in Practice

1) 병원 접수창구에서 사용할 수 있는 표현
Useful expressions at the reception desk.

① 저는 장미영 박사님께 진료 받아요.

Dr. Jang Mi-young is my doctor.

② 저는 김철수 박사님을 만나러 왔어요.

I'd like to see Dr. Kim Cheol-soo.

③ 미리 예약전화를 했어요.

I've already made an appointment with the doctor by phone.

④ 예약 안 했어요. I don't have an appointment.

⑤ 외래접수를 하고 싶어요. I'd like to register as an outpatient.

⑥ 진료/건강검진을 받으러 왔어요.

I'd like to see a doctor/ get a physical exam.

2) 어디로 가요? / Where should I go?

① 임신 했어요. 어디로 가요? I'm pregnant. Where should I go?

② 아기가 아파요. 어디로 가요? My baby is sick. Where should I go?

③ 이가 아파요. 어디로 가요? I have a toothache. Where should I go?

④ 눈이 아파요. 어디로 가요? My eye is sore. Where should I go?

⑤ 귀가 아파요. 어디로 가요? I have an earache. Where should I go?

⑥ 피부가 가려워요. 어디로 가요?

I have a problem with my skin. Where should I go?

⑦ 코가 아파요. 어디로 가요?

I have a problem with my nose. Where should I go?

⑧ 항문이 아파요. 어디로 가요?

I have a pain in my anus. Where should I go?

⑨ 머리가 아파요. 어디로 가요?

I have a headache. Where should I go?

Medical Korean for English Speakers

II. 진료를 원할 때
Medical Treatment

05 병원 응급실
Emergency Room

1. 핵심어 Key Words

1) 응급실 Emergency Room (ER)

2) 응급 입원실 Emergent Patient Room

3) 응급 처치 First Aid Treatment

4) 응급 치료 Emergency Treatment

5) 환자 Patient

6) 의사 선생님 Doctor

7) 간호사 Nurse

8) 입원 Hospitalization

9) 퇴원 Discharge from the Hospital

10) 양식 Forms

11) 진단서 Diagnosis

12) 동의서 Written Consent

13) 국민건강보험 National Health Insurance

14) 수혈 Blood Transfusion

15) 주사 쇼크 Injection Shock

2. 단어 Words

1) '응급실'이 뭐예요? What is 'an emergency room[*Eunggeupshil*]?'

① '응급실'이란 병원에서 환자의 응급 처치를 할 수 있는 설비를 갖추어 놓은 곳이에요. An emergency room[*Eunggeupshil*] is one of the facilities in a hospital, where a patient can receive first-aid.

② '응급'이란 급한 상황에 대처하는 것이에요.
"Emergency[*Eunggeup*]" is an unexpected urgent situation.

③ '처치'란 어떤 사건에 대하여 알맞은 조치를 취하는 것이에요.
"Treatment[*Cheochi*]" is taking measures for an accident or an event.

④ '조치'란 어떤 문제를 잘 살펴서 필요한 대책을 세우는 것이에요.
"Taking measures[*Jochi*]" means preparing for a countermeasure against a specific problem.

⑤ '대책'이란 어떤 문제를 해결하는 수단이에요.
"Countermeasure[*Daechaek*]" is a way to solve a problem.

⑥ '수단'이란 어떤 목적을 이루기 위한 방법이에요.
"A Way[*Sudan*]" is a methodology to achieve a goal.

⑦ '설비'란 필요한 것을 준비해 놓은 것이에요. "Equipment[*Seolbi*]" is a set of necessary materials prepared for a specific purpose.

2) '응급 입원실'이 뭐예요?

What is 'an emergent patient's room[*Eunggeup Ibwonshil*]'?

① '응급 입원실'이란 환자가 급하게 병원에 들어가서 머무는 방이 에요. "An emergent patient's room[*Eunggeup Ipwonshil*]" is a special room in a hospital for an emergent patient to stay temporarily.

② '입원'이란 환자가 일정한 기간 동안 병원에 들어가 머무는 일 이에요. "Hospitalization[*Ipwon*]" is a process for a patient to stay in a hospital for a specified period of time.

3) '환자'가 뭐예요? What is "a patient[*Hwanja*]"?

'환자'란 병들거나 다쳐서 치료를 받아야 할 사람을 말해요.

'A patient[*Hwanja*]' is a person who seeks medical treatment.

4) '응급 처치'가 뭐예요? What is "First Aid[*Eunggeup Cheochi*]"?

① '응급 처치'란 '응급 치료'라고도 해요.

"First aid[*Eunggeup Cheochi*]" can also be called "urgent treatment".

② '응급 처치'란 갑작스런 상처에 대하여 위험한 고비를 넘기기 위하여 임시로 하는 치료에요. "First aid[*Eunggeup Cheochi*]" is a temporary medical treatment for an emergent injury.

③ '응급 치료'란 갑작스런 병에 대하여 위험한 고비를 넘기기 위 하여 임시로 하는 치료에요. "Urgent treatment[*Eunggeup Chiryo*]" is a temporary medical solution for an emergent disease.

④ '고비'란 막다른 단계를 말해요. "A critical point[*Gobi*]" is the most dangerous stage for a patient.

⑤ '위험한 고비'란 위험으로 인해 죽기 직전의 막다른 상황을 말

해요. "A dangerous critical point[*Wiheomhan Gobi*]" is the final stage before the death for a patient.

5) '경기'가 뭐예요? What is "Convulsions[*Gyeonggi*]"?

① '경기'는 갑작스럽게 깜짝 깜짝 놀라는 증상이에요. "Convulsions[*Gyeonggi*]" is a symptom of violent shaking of the body after being repeatedly suprised.

② '경기를 일으키다'는 말은 깜짝 놀라는 증상이에요. "Being convulsed[*Gyeonggirul Irukida*]" is being startled.

③ '경기'는 [경끼]라고 발음해요. "Convulsion" is pronounced as [gjʌŋggi].

6) '경련'이 뭐예요? What is "Cramp[*Gyeongnyeon*]"?

① '경련'은 몸의 근육이 급격하게 수축과 이완을 반복하는 증상이에요. "Cramp[*Gyeongnyeon*]" is a rapid repetition of contraction and relaxation of muscles.

　㉠ '수축'은 몸이 오그라드는 모양이에요. "Contraction[*Suchuk*]" is s tightening of body muscle.

　㉡ '오그라들다'는 몸의 부피가 작아지는 모양을 말해요. "Shrinking[*Ogradulda*]" is tightening.

　㉢ '이완'은 몸이 퍼지는 모양이에요. "Relaxation[*Iwan*]" is the relaxation of muscles and body.

　㉣ '퍼지다'는 몸의 부피가 커지는 모양을 말해요. "Stretched [*Pyeojida*]" means expanding.

② '경련을 일으키다'는 말은 몸을 떠는 증상을 말해요. "Being

convulsed" means "trembling of the body".

7) '오한'이 뭐예요? What is "having chills[*Ohan*]"?

   ① '오한'은 몸이 춥고 떨리는 증상이에요. "Having chills[*Ohan*]" is 'the body trembling with cold'.

   ② '오한이 난다'고 말해요. We say, "I have chills[*Ohani nanda*]."

8) '오심'이 뭐예요? What is 'nausea[*Oshim*]'?

   ① '오심'은 구역질이 나지만 토하지는 않고 신물만 올라오는 증상이에요. 'Nausea[*Oshim*]' is the condition of having acid reflux without vomiting.

   ② '오심'은 배 멀미를 하거나 차멀미가 나서 속이 울렁거리는 증세를 말해요. 'Nausea[*Oshim*]' is a sickness similar with carsickness or seasickness.

   ③ '배 멀미'란 배를 타고 있을 때 속이 울렁거리거나 토하는 것을 말해요. 'Seasickness[*Baemeolmi*]' is a feeling of needing to vomit or feeling sick because of the way the boat is moving.

   ④ '차멀미'란 자동차, 버스, 트럭 등을 타고 있을 때 속이 울렁거리거나 토하는 것을 말해요. 'Carsickness[*Chameolmi*]' is a feeling of needing to vomit or feeling sick because of the motion produced by riding a car.

9) '신물'이 뭐예요? What is acid reflux[*Shinmul*]?

   ① '신물'은 음식에 체했을 때 복으로 넘어오는 시큼한 물이에요. 'Acid reflux[*Shinmul*]' is sour liquid from the stomach as a result of indigestion.

② '신물이 넘어 온다'고 말해요.

We say, "I have acid reflux[*Shinmul Neomeo Onda*]".

③ '신물이 올라 온다'고 말해요

We also say, "The acid reflux comes up from the stomach[*Shinmul Olla Onda*]".

④ '신물이 난다'라고 하면 하기 싫은 일을 오래해서 이제는 하기 싫다는 뜻이에요. It also means, "I am sick and tired of something. [*Shinmul i nanda*]"

10) '출혈'이 뭐예요? What is 'bleeding[*Choolhyeol*]'?

① '출혈'은 피가 혈관 밖으로 나오는 것을 말해요.

'Bleeding[*Choolhyeol*]' is the leaking of blood out of the blood vessel.

② '출혈 과다'란 피가 많이 난 상태를 말해요.

'Copious bleeding[*Chulhyeol Gwada*]' means excessive bleeding.

11) '지혈'이 뭐예요? What is 'hemostasis[*Jihyeol*]'?

'지혈'이란 나오던 피가 멈추는 것을 말해요.

'Hemostasis[*Jihyeol*]' is the stopping of bleeding.

12) '빈혈'이 뭐예요? What is 'anemia[*Binhyeol*]'?

① '빈혈'이란 혈액 내의 적혈구나 헤모글로빈 감소로 현기증이 일어나는 증세를 말해요.

'Anemia[*Binheol*]' is having sense of vertigo due to the decrease of red blood cells or hemoglobin in the blood.

② '현기증'이란 어지럼증을 말해요.

'Vertigo[*Hyeongijeung*]' is feeling dizzy.

13) '통증'이 뭐예요? What is ache?

'통증'이란 심하게 아픈 증세예요.

'Ache[*Tongjeung*]' is severe pain.

14) '토사곽란'[토사광난]이 뭐예요?

What is acute gastroenteritis[*Tosagwangnan*]?

'토사곽란'이란 입으로는 토하고 아래로는 설사하면서 배가 아픈 병이에요.

'Acute gastroenteritis[*Tosagwangnan*]' is a severe stomachache accompanied by vomiting and diarrhea.

3. 유용한 표현 Useful Expressions

1) 어떤 증상이 있을 때 '응급실'에 가요?

When should you go to the emergency room?

You should go to the emergency room when …

① 열이 39°C가 넘으면 응급실에 가요.

the body temperature goes over 39 degrees Celsius.

② 갑자기 눈에 초점이 없으면 응급실에 가요.

your pupils dilate all of a sudden.

③ 갑자기 숨을 못 쉬면 응급실에 가요.

you can't breath all of a sudden.

④ 갑자기 몸이 뻣뻣하게 굳으면 응급실에 가요.

your body gets stiffened on a sudden.

⑤ 갑자기 온 몸을 쭉 뻗고 바들바들 떨면 응급실에 가요.

the body gets stiffened and trembles on a sudden.

⑥ 경기[경끼]가 심하면 응급실에 가요.

a baby is convulsing.

⑦ 심하게 경련을 일으키면 응급실에 가요.

you have a severe cramp.

⑧ 출혈이 심하면 응급실에 가요.

you bleed too much.

⑨ 지혈이 안 되면 응급실에 가요.

you cannot stop bleeding.

⑩ 갑자기 빈혈이 일어나면 응급실에 가요.

you have a sudden symptom of anemia.

⑪ 갑자기 가슴 통증을 호소하면 응급실에 가요.

you have a sudden chest pain.

⑫ 야간에 출산 증세가 있으면 응급실에 가요.

you are giving birth to a baby.

⑬ 교통사고로 심하게 다친 사람이 있으면 응급실에 데려다 줘요.

you see a person who is severely injured in a traffic accident.

⑭ 목에 가시가 걸리면 응급실에 가요.

you get a fishbone stuck in your throat.

⑮ 몸에 갑자기 이물질이 들어갔는데, 빼기 어려우면 응급실에 가요.

you find a foreign body, which cannot be removed.

2) 열이 39°C 이상이 되면 어떻게 응급처치 해요?

What should we do when a person has a high fever over 39 degrees celsius?

① 열이 높으면 해열제를 먹여요. You should provide a fever reducer.

② 옷을 벗기고 시원하게 해요. Take off the person's clothes and cool him down.

③ 따뜻한 물(35~37°C)을 수건에 적셔 몸을 닦아요. Wipe the whole body with warmly wet towel(35~37°C).

④ 물수건으로 쉬지 않고 몸을 닦아요. Continuously wipe the whole body with a wet towel.

⑤ 몸을 여러 번 닦은 후 얇은 옷을 입혀요. Wipe the body several times and clothe the patient lightly.

⑥ 물을 마시게 해요. Give the patient some water.

⑦ 몸을 떨면 물수건을 사용하지 않아요. If the patient trembles, don't use the wet towel.

⑧ 몸을 떨면 꼭 안아줘요. If the patient continuously trembles, hug him or her.

⑨ 전화 119로 도움을 청해요. Call 119 for further help.

3) '눈에 초점이 없다'는 말이 뭐예요? What does "dilating pupil" mean?

'눈에 초점이 없다'는 말은 정신을 잃었다는 뜻이에요.

It means that the patient becomes unconscious.

4) '몸이 뻣뻣하게 굳었다'는 말이 뭐예요?

What does "getting stiffened" mean?

'몸이 뻣뻣하게 굳었다'는 말은 몸이 경직되었다는 뜻이에요.

"The body is stiffened" means the body is hard.

4. 현장 한국어 Korean in Practice

1) 응급실에서는 이렇게 말하세요. Say the followings in an emergency room.

① 열이 39°C가 넘어서 왔어요. I'm here because the patient's temperature is over 39 degrees celsius.

② 열이 나고 눈에 초점이 없어요. The patient has a fever and his pupils dilated.

③ 갑자기 숨을 안 쉬어요. The patient is not breathing.

④ 갑자기 몸이 뻣뻣하게 굳었어요. The patient's body is stiff.

⑤ 갑자기 온 몸을 쭉 뻗고 바들바들 떨었어요. The patient stretched out and trembled very hard.

⑥ 경기[경끼]가 심해요. The patient has severe convulsions.

⑦ 심하게 경련을 일으키면서 쓰러졌어요. The patient fell down after a severe cramp.

⑧ 출혈이 심해요. The patient is bleeding a lot.

⑨ 지혈이 안돼요. The bleeding will not stop.

⑩ 빈혈을 일으켰어요. The patient is anemic.

⑪ 갑자기 가슴 통증을 호소하더니 쓰러졌어요. The patient complained of chest pain and fell down.

⑫ 갑자기 출산 기미가 보였어요. She shows a sudden sign of childbirth.

⑬ 교통사고가 났어요. I was in a traffic accident.

⑭ 목에 가시가 걸렸어요. I have a fishbone stuck in my throat.

⑮ 동전을 삼켰어요. I swallowed a coin.

2) '다리가 부러졌을 때' 어떻게 말해요?

How can I express that I have a broken leg?

① "오른쪽 다리가 부러졌어요." "My right leg is broken."

② "왼쪽 다리가 부러졌어요." "My left leg is broken."

3) '팔이 빠졌을 때' 어떻게 말해요?

How can I express that my arms have come out of their joints?

① "오른쪽 팔이 빠졌어요." "My right arm is out of its joint."

② "왼쪽 팔이 빠졌어요." "My left arm is out of its joint."

4) '갈비뼈가 부러졌을 때' 어떻게 말해요?

How can I express that I broke my ribs?

① "오른쪽 갈비뼈가 부러졌어요." "Some of the ribs on my right side are broken."

② "왼쪽 갈비뼈가 부러졌어요." "Some of the ribs on my left side are broken."

▶ 이물질 A foreign body
'이물질'이란 정상적이 아닌 다른 물건을 말한다.
'A foreign body' is something that does not belong to the body.

5) 몸속에 이물질이 들어갔을 때 어떻게 말해요?

How can I express that I have a 'foreign body' in my body?

① 100원짜리 동전을 삼켰어요. He swallowed a 100 won coin.

② 바늘을 삼켰어요. He swallowed a needle.

③ 바늘에 찔렸어요. I was stuck with a needle.

④ 발바닥에 못이 박혔어요. There is a nail in my foot.

⑤ 손바닥에 가시가 박혔어요 I pricked my hand on a thorn.

⑥ 허벅지에 총알이 박혔어요. There is a bullet in my thigh.

6) 동물이나 벌레에 의해 다쳤을 때 어떻게 말해요?

How can I express that I was injured by an animal or a bug?

① 멧돼지한테 물렸어요. I was bitten by a wild boar.

② 뱀한테 물렸어요. I was bitten by a snake.

③ 벌에 쏘였어요. I was stung by a bee.

④ 개한테 물렸어요. I was bitten by a dog.

⑤ 소뿔에 받쳤어요. I was gored by a bull.

⑥ 말한테 밟혔어요. I was stepped on by a horse.

⑦ 말에서 떨어졌어요. I fell off a horse.

⑧ 닭한테 쪼였어요. I was pecked by a hen.

7) 설사 응급처치 Emergency Treatment for Diarrhea

① 따뜻하게 자고, 안정을 취한다. Take a nap in a warm place and rest.

② 음식물에 의한 설사는 먹은 음식을 모두 토하도록 한다. If the diarrhea is caused by ingested food, the patient should throw up every food that he or she has eaten.

③ 탈수현상을 예방하기 위하여 따뜻한 물을 마신다.

In order to avoid dehydration, the patient should drink plenty of warm water.

④ 음식을 먹지 않거나 식사량을 줄인다.

The patient should not eat any food or reduce the amount of food consumed.

⑤ 만성설사는 의사와 상담하여 치료를 받는다.

If you are having chronic diarrhea, talk to your doctor and seek treatment.

8) 식중독 응급처치 Emergency Treatment for Food Poisoning

① 소금물을 마셔서 음식물을 모두 토하도록 한다.

The patient should drink salt water and throw up everything (s)he ate.

② 음식을 먹지 않는다.

The patient should not eat anything.

③ 몸을 따뜻하게 한다. 특히 배와 발을 따뜻하게 해야 한다.

The patient should be kept warm, especially their abdomen and feet.

④ 링거, 포도당 주사, 강심제 등을 맞는다.

The patient should have some intravenous(IV) injection.

⑤ 병원으로 이송한다.

The patient should be sent to the hospital.

9) 출혈이 심할 때 In Case of Serious Bleeding

① 붕대를 두껍게 대고 단단하게 매어준다.

A thick bandage should be tightly pressed against the wound.

② 출혈부를 심장보다 높게 하고 얼음을 댄다.

The bleeding wound should be placed higher than heart, and an ice bag should be applied.

③ 솟는 출혈이면 심장에 가까운 동맥을 손으로 강하게 누른다.

If the blood is spurting, press down on the artery on the side of the wound closer to the heart.

④ 머리가 흔들리지 않도록 한다.

Make sure the patient's head remains still.

10) 고열 응급처치 Emergency Treatment for High Fever

① 조용히 절대안정을 취한다.

The patient should be kept calm and relax.

② 몸을 따뜻하게 유지하고 땀이 나면 옷을 갈아입는다.

The patient should keep himself warm and change into dry clothes if (s)he is sweating.

③ 음주, 흡연, 목욕, 운동을 삼간다.

The patient should avoid drinking alcohol, smoking, bathing, and exercising.

④ 소화가 잘 되는 음식을 섭취한다.

The patient should eat easily digestable foods.

⑤ 비타민 C를 섭취한다.

The patient should take vitamin C.

⑥ 병원으로 이송한다.

The patient should be taken to the hospital.

11) 뇌졸중으로 쓰러질 때 In Case of Falling During a Stroke

① 쓰러진 상태로 조용히 자게 한다.

Leave the patient to sleep calmly.

② 이름을 부르거나 어깨를 흔들면 안 된다.

You should not call the patient's name or shake him/her awake.

③ 의사가 올 때까지 절대 안정을 취한다.

Let the patient relax until the doctor comes.

④ 복장을 느슨하게 하고 호흡을 편하게 한다.

Loosen the patient's clothes and help him/her breathe with ease.

⑤ 추운 곳이면 4명 정도의 인원을 동원하여 따뜻한 곳으로 옮긴다.

If it is too cold, move the patient to a warmer place with the help of other people.

⑥ 목과 머리가 움직이지 않도록 한다.

Be careful not to move the patient's head or neck.

12) 머리를 강하게 부딪쳤을 때 In Case of Patients Bumping their Heads

① 우선 안정을 취한다.

Stabilize the patient.

② 머리에 찬물 찜질을 한다.

Give the patient a cold pack to put on the head.

③ 머리 부상은 후유증이 남기 쉽다.

The injury to the head will be accompanied by side effects.

④ 빠른 시간 내에 병원으로 이송한다.

Take the patient to the hospital as soon as possible.

13) 뇌빈혈로 쓰러졌을 때 In Case of Cerebral Anemia

① 실내인 경우는 창문을 열고 환기시킨다.

If it occurs indoors, open a window to allow some fresh air in.

② 실외인 경우는 나무 그늘로 옮긴다.

If it occurs outdoors, move the patients into the shade.

③ 강한 산, 암모니아 냄새로 코를 자극한다.

Stimulate the patient's nose with smells of strong acid and ammonia.

④ 콧구멍을 계속 간지럽힌다.

Stimulate the patient's nasal vacancy continuously.

⑤ 의식이 회복되면 술, 커피 등 흥분성 음료를 마시게 해도 좋다.

If the patient awakes, have him drink some excitable drinks such as alcohol, coffee.

⑥ 가능한 빨리 깨우도록 한다.

Try to wake the patient as quickly as possible.

14) 심장이 멎어 쓰러졌을 때 In Case of a Heart Attack

① 몸을 위로 향하게 한 후 자게 한다.

Have the patient sit up and sleep.

② 맥이 멎어 있는지 확인한다.

Check the patient's pulse.

③ 심장 마사지를 한다.

Massage the patient's chest.

④ 인공호흡을 병행한다.

Artificially ventilate the patient.

15) 멀미 응급처치 In Case of Car Sickness

① 창문을 열어 환기를 시킨다.

Open a window for ventilation.

② 버스를 탈 때 앞 좌석에 앉도록 한다.

Sit in the front seats instead of the back seats.

③ 먼 곳을 바라본다.

Focus on more distant objects.

④ 넥타이를 푼다.

Take off your necktie.

⑤ 벨트를 느슨하게 맨다.

Loosen your belt.

16) 눈 응급처치 유형 In Case of Eye Problems

① 눈에 화학 물질이 들어갔을 때

When chemicals get into the eye,

㉠ 다친 눈을 흐르는 물에 대고 10분 이상 그대로 있는다.

Rinse the contaminated eye with running water for 10 minutes.

㉡ 위아래 눈꺼풀을 잘 씻는다.

Wash the eyelids well.

㉢ 통증으로 눈을 뜨지 못하는 경우에는 조심스럽고 강하게 눈을 벌려 준다. When a patient cannot open their eyes due to pain, you should try to gently force the eye open.

㉣ 경련으로 눈이 안 떠지는 경우에는 조심스럽고 강하게 눈을 벌려 준다. When a patient cannot open their eyes because of a twitch, you should try to gently open the eye with care.

㉤ 소독 안대나 깨끗하고 보풀이 없는 수건으로 눈을 가린다.

Bandage the eye with a sterilized eye patch.

㉥ 병원으로 이송한다.

Take the patient to a hospital.

② 눈에 이물질이 들어갔을 때 In Case of Eyewinker

㉠ 이물질이 들어간 눈만 흐르는 물에 10분 이상 그대로 놓아둔다.

An eye with an eyewinker should be washed with running water over 10 minutes.

ⓛ 눈을 비비지 않는다.

Do not rub your eyes.

ⓒ 눈을 만지기 전에 손을 깨끗이 씻는다.

Wash your hands before you touch your eye.

ⓔ 눈꺼풀을 당기며 젖힌 후 물 묻힌 면봉으로 이물질을 빼낸다.

Pull the eyelid and take out the eyewinker with a cotton swab.

ⓜ 눈이 빨개지고 눈물이 나면 가능한 빨리 병원으로 간다.

If the eye gets red and teary, go to a hospital as quickly as possible.

ⓗ 눈에 쇳가루가 들어갔을 때는 최대한 빨리 병원으로 간다.

If iron filings get into your eye, go to a hospital as quickly as possible.

③ 눈 주위 피부가 찢어져 피가 날 때

If the skin around your eye is bleeding,

ⓖ 상처 부위를 노출시킨다.

Leave the wound exposed and open to air.

ⓛ 상처 부위를 붕대나 수건으로 덮지 않는다.

Do not cover the wound with bandages or towels.

ⓒ 상처 밑에서 흐르는 피를 닦는다.

Wipe away the blood under the wound.

ⓔ 병원으로 이송한다.

Take the patient to a hospital.

④ 갑자기 눈이 안 보일 때. In Case of Sudden Blindness

ⓖ 눈을 감고 안정을 취한다.

Close and rest the affected eyes.

ⓛ 비타민 A를 보충하기 위해 시원한 당근 주스를 마신다.

Drink cool carrot juice because it has lots of vitamin A.

ⓒ 서서히 눈을 뜬다.

Open your eyes slowly.

17) 귀 응급처치 유형 Emergency Treatment for the Ear

① 귀에 이물질이 들어갔을 때

If something goes into your ear

ㄱ 귀에 벌레가 들어갔다면 손전등을 켜서 귀에 갖다 대준다.

If an insect goes into your ear, turn on a flashlight and put the light toward the earhole.

ㄴ 면봉에 식용유 같은 식물성 기름을 묻혀 귓구멍 주변에 발라 준다.

Apply some vegetable oil around the patient's earhole.

ㄷ 단추, 콩 등 딱딱한 물건이 들어갔다면 빨리 병원으로 이송 한다.

If something hard, such as a button or a pea, enter the earhole, the patient should be carried to the hospital.

② 귀가 아플 때 In Case of Ear Pain

ㄱ 비행 중 귀에 통증이 있을 때는 하품을 하거나 껌을 씹는다.

If you have a pressure in the ear during a flight, yawn or chew gum.

ㄴ 비행 중 귀에 통증이 있을 때는 코를 손으로 잡은 다음 입 안 가득 공기를 들이마신 후 입을 다문 채 입안의 공기를 코 로 불어내듯이 하여 고막을 밖으로 밀리게 한다.

If you have a pressure in the ear during a flight, pinch the nose shut with a hand, inhale some air and try to blow out the air with the mouth closed, so that the eardrum may be stimulated.

ⓒ 비행 중에 있는 어린아이에게는 우유를 먹이거나 인공 젖꼭지를 빨도록 한다.

If an infant is riding a plane, they should be provided with milk or an artificial nipple.

ⓔ 물놀이 후 귀에 통증이 있을 때는 귀를 아래 방향으로 향하게 한 후 가볍게 머리를 흔들어 물을 뺀다.

If you have water in your ear after swimming, turn the affected ear downward toward the ground and gently shake your head to get the water out.

ⓜ 물놀이 후 귀에 통증이 있을 때는 면봉으로 귀의 입구를 닦아 주고 물기를 없애 준다.

If you have water in your ear after swimming, wipe the entrance of your earhole with a cotton swab to dry the ear.

18) 중독 응급처치 Emergency Treatment for Poisoning

① 약물 중독 Medicinal Poisoning

ㄱ 독물의 흡수를 지연시키기 위해 우유를 마시게 한다.

Have the patient drink milk to delay the absorption of the poison.

ㄴ 독물의 흡수를 지연시키기 위해 생계란을 먹게 한다.

Have the patient eat a raw egg to delay the absorption of the poison.

ㄷ 독물의 흡수를 지연시키기 위해 밀가루 탄 물을 마시게 한다.

Have the patient drink some water and flour to delay the

absorption of the poison.

ⓔ 중독물이 담겨 있던 용기, 구토물을 가지고 병원으로 간다.

Take the poison's container and any vomit produced by the patient after ingesting the poison to the hospital.

ⓜ 중독 원인, 중독 시간, 중독 양을 파악하는 것이 좋다.

Verify the cause, duration, and amount of poison.

② 수면제 중독 Sleeping Pill Poisoning

ⓐ 환자가 의식이 있으면 바로 토하게 한다.

If the patient is conscious, allow him/her to vomit.

ⓑ 환자가 의식이 없으면 편하게 눕게 한다.

If the patient is unconscious, place him/her in side-lying position.

ⓒ 환자의 호흡이 멎어 있으면 곧바로 인공호흡을 한다.

If the patient is not breathing, begin mouth-to-mouth resuscitation.

ⓓ 환자를 최대한 빨리 병원으로 데려간다.

Take the patient to the hospital as quickly as possible.

③ 복어 중독 Swell-fish Poisoning

ⓐ 환자를 최대한 빨리 병원으로 데려간다.

Take the patient to the hospital as quickly as possible.

ⓑ 호흡마비가 오면 인공호흡을 한다.

If the patient can't breathe, try mouth-to-mouth resuscitation.

④ 가스 중독 Gas Poisoning

ⓐ 창문을 열어 바깥 공기가 많이 들어오게 한다.

Open the windows for ventilation.

ⓑ 환자를 구조할 때는 반드시 두 사람 이상이 필요하다.

At least two people are needed to rescue the patient.

ⓒ 둘 이상이 환자를 구조할 때는 한 사람은 밖에 있고 방 안으로 들어가는 사람은 허리에 밧줄을 매고 들어간다.

If more than two people are rescuing the patient, only one rescuer will enter the gas filled room. The entering rescuer will tie a rope around his/her waist and the other end of the rope will remain outside with the other rescuers.

ⓔ 환자를 구조할 때 방안으로 들어가는 사람은 숨을 잠깐 멈추고 최대한 재빨리 환자를 끌어낸다.

The rescuer who is entering the room should hold his/her breath, and evacuate the patient as quickly as possible.

ⓜ 환자를 신선한 공기가 있는 곳으로 끌어낸다.

Take the patient to a non-contaminated place with fresh air.

ⓗ 환자가 춥지 않도록 하반신을 담요로 덮어준다.

Cover lower half of the patient's body with a blanket so that the patient does not get cold.

ⓢ 환자가 의식을 잃지 않도록 큰 소리로 이름을 부른다.

Call the patient's name so that the patient does not slip into unconsciousness.

ⓞ 환자의 코에 암모니아수를 대준다.

Place an ammonia stick near the patient's nose to arouse him/her.

ⓩ 환자가 의식을 회복하면 레몬수나 따뜻한 커피를 마시게 한다.

When the patient becomes aroused, provide him/her with lemon water or coffee.

⑤ 버섯 중독 Mushroom Poisoning

ⓐ 목구멍에 손가락을 넣어 토하게 한다.

Have the patient try to vomit.

ⓛ 빨리 의사의 진단과 치료를 받아야 한다.

Take the patient to a doctor as quickly as possible.

⑥ 급성 알코올 중독 Acute Alcohol Poisoning

㉠ 몸을 따뜻하게 한다.

Warm the patient.

ⓛ 편안한 자세로 눕게 한다.

Place the patient in a comfortable posture.

㉢ 호흡이 용이하도록 의복을 느슨하게 늦춘다.

Loosen the patient's clothing to allow for easier breathing.

㉣ 환자가 토하면 얼굴을 옆으로 돌려 목이 막히지 않도록 한다.

If the patient vomits, turn his/her head to the side so that he/she does not choke.

⑦ 농약 중독 Agricultural Chemical Poisoning

㉠ 농약의 상표를 보고 농약의 종류를 확인한다.

Identify the kind of agricultural chemical poisoning by checking the brand name.

ⓛ 농약 먹은 시간을 확인한다.

Verify the time that the patient was exposed to the agricultural chemicals.

㉢ 농약의 상표에 응급처치 안내가 있을 경우 지시에 따른다.

If you find first-aid directions on the brand label, follow those directions.

㉣ 119에 전화를 걸어 농약의 종류를 말하고 지시에 따른다.

Call 119, tell the emergency responder the kind of agricultural chemicals ingested/you were exposed to, and then follow the emergency responder's directions.

ⓜ 물을 마시게 한 후 목구멍에 손가락을 넣어 토하게 한다.

Have the patient drink water and then try to vomit.

ⓗ 환자가 의식이 있으면 심호흡을 하게 한다.

If the patient is conscious, have him/her take a deep breath.

ⓢ 환자가 의식이 없으면 인공호흡을 한다.

If the patient is unconscious, begin manual/mechanical ventiliation.

ⓞ 농약이 묻은 피부는 아주 많은 양의 물에 15분 이상 담근다.

Any skin contaminated by agricultural chemicals should be rinsed within water for more than 15 minutes.

ⓩ 농약이 묻었던 옷은 따로 세탁하거나 버린다.

Any clothes contaminated by agricultural chemicals should be washed separately or thrown away.

ⓧ 환자의 입에 고여 있는 침을 닦아내거나 머리를 옆으로 하여 침이 입 밖으로 쉽게 나오도록 해준다.

The spit in the patient's mouth should be removed clearly.

19) 응급실 대화 Conversations in the Emergency Room

* 의사 Doctor

① 예전에도 이런 적이 있었나요?

Have you ever experienced this before?

② 예전에는 어느 병원을 다니셨나요?

Which hospitals have you been before?

③ 지난번과 같은 증상인가요?

Do you have the same symptoms as you had before?

④ 지난번에는 어땠어요?

How was it the other time?

⑤ 보호자에게 연락해 주세요.

Please contact the patient's guardian.

⑥ 다른 병원으로 가시겠습니까?

Would you like to go to another hospital?

⑦ 다니시던 병원으로 옮기시겠습니까?

Would you like to move to the hospital you were at previously?

⑧ 조금 더 상황을 지켜보실래요? 아니면 다른 큰 병원으로 옮기시 겠습니까?

Would you like us to observe the situation more, or would you like to move to a bigger hospital?

⑨ 구급차를 불러드릴까요?

Shall I call an ambulance for you?

⑩ 어느 분이 같이 따라가실 건가요?

Which one of you will be accompanying the patient?

⑪ 혈압과 맥박은 정상입니다.

The blood pressure and pulse are normal.

⑫ 상황을 조금 두고 지켜봐야하겠습니다.

We'd better take a look a little more.

⑬ 담당 선생님이 오늘 비번입니다.

The doctor in charge is off-duty today.

⑭ 어제 담당했던 선생님이 교대하셔서 다른 선생님이 치료하고 계 십니다.

The doctor who took care of the patient yesterday has changed shifts. Another doctor is treating the patient today.

⑮ 다른 검사를 좀 해봐야겠습니다.

We need to do more tests.

⑯ 먼저 접수를 해주시겠습니까?

Could you register first?

⑰ 지금부터 엑스레이를 찍고 피 검사를 하겠습니다.

Now, we are going to take an X-ray and draw blood for a blood test.

⑱ CT 촬영을 하겠습니다.

We will take a CT scan.

⑲ MRI 촬영을 하겠습니다.

We will do an MRI.

⑳ 옷을 다 벗어 주세요.

Take off all of your clothes.

㉑ 계속 주물러 주세요.

Continuously massage the patient.

㉒ 계속 잡고 계세요.

Keep holding the patient.

㉓ 자꾸 말을 걸어 주세요.

Keep speaking to the patient.

㉔ 아직 의식이 돌아오지 않고 있습니다.

The patient hasn't regained consciousness yet.

㉕ 맥박과 호흡 상태를 보겠습니다.

Let me check the pulse and breathing.

㉖ 영양주사를 놓겠습니다.

Let me give an intravenous tonic injection to the patient.

㉗ 링겔이 다 떨어지면 얘기하세요.

Let me know when the I.V. is done.

㉘ 지금 먹던 약은 어떻게 하나요?

What should I do with the medication I've taken so far?

㉙ 상황이 좋아지지 않으면 전기 충격기를 사용해 보겠습니다.

If the situation doesn't get better, let me try electric shock therapy

㉚ 초음파 검사를 했으나 오진으로 판명되었습니다.

We had an ultrasonic examination, but it was proved to be a wrong diagnosis.

* 보호자 Guardian

① 응급실에 보호자도 같이 대기해야 하나요?

Does the guardian have to wait in the Emergency Room?

② 담당 의사 선생님 성함이 어떻게 되시나요?

What is the name of the doctor in charge?

③ 환자의 기록을 좀 보고 싶습니다.

I'd like to see the patient's record.

④ 환자의 기록이 남아 있는지요?

Do you have the patient's record?

⑤ 호흡곤란으로 갑자기 쓰러졌습니다.

The patient was having difficulty breathing and then fell down all of a sudden.

06

내과
Internal Medicine Department

1. 핵심어 Key Words

1) 내과 Internal Medicine

2) 소화기 Digestive Organs

3) 순환기 Circulative Organs

4) 호흡기 Respiratory Organ

5) 신장 Kidney

6) 식중독 Food Poisoning

7) 구토 Vomit

8) 복통 Stomachache

9) 감기 Cold

10) 흉통 Chest pain

2. 단어 Words

1) 내과가 뭐예요? What is "the Department of Internal Medicine"[*Naegwa*]?

내과는 내장 기관에 생긴 병을 수술 없이 고치는 병원 부서 이름이에요.

"The department of Internal Medicine" is the name of a department in a hospital that treats diseases of the internal organs without using surgery.

2) 내과에는 무엇이 있어요? What makes up the department of Internal Medicine?

내과에는 ① 소화기, ② 순환기, ③ 호흡기, ④ 신장, ⑤ 내분비계, ⑥ 알러지, ⑦ 류마티스, ⑧ 감염, ⑨ 혈액 종양 등이 있어요.

The department of Internal Medicine is composed of the following sub-departments. ① gastroenterology, ② circulation, ③ pulmonology, ④ nephrology, ⑤ endocrinology & metabolism, ⑥ allergy, ⑦ rheumatology, ⑧ infectious diseases and ⑨ hematology & oncology.

3) 소화기가 뭐예요? What is the Gastroenteric System[*Sohwagi*]?

① 소화기란 음식물을 소화하는 기관이에요. The gastroenteric orgains are the organs that are related to the digestion of food.

② 소화기에는 ㉠ 구강, ㉡ 식도, ㉢ 위, ㉣ 장, ㉤ 항문, ㉥ 침샘, ㉦ 간 등이 있어요.

In the gastroenteric system, there is the ㉠ mouth, ㉡ esophagus, ㉢ stomach, ㉣ intestines, ㉤ anus, ㉥ salivary gland, ㉦ liver.

③ 소화기 질환이란 소화기에 생긴 병을 말해요.

Gastroenteric diseases are those that occur in the digestive system.

④ 소화기 질환이 있으면 소화기 내과에 가요.

If you have a gastroenteric diseases, you should go to the hospital's internal medicine department.

4) 순환기가 뭐예요? What is the Circulatory System[*Sunhwangi*]?

① 순환기란 혈액을 순환시키는 기관이에요.

The circulatory system includes all the organs in the body that help to circulate blood.

② 순환기에는 ㉠ 심장, ㉡ 혈관, ㉢ 림프관 등이 있어요.

In the circulatory system, there are the heart, blood vessels, and the lymphatic system.

③ 순환기 질환이란 순환기에 생긴 병을 말해요.

Circulatory diseases are those that occur in the circulatory system.

④ 순환기 질환이 있으면 순환기 내과에 가요.

If you have a circulatory disease, you should go to the hospital's internal medicine department.

⑤ 순환기 질환에는 ㉠ 뇌졸중, ㉡ 동맥경화, ㉢ 심근경색, ㉣ 부정맥, ㉤ 요통, ㉥ 고혈압, ㉦ 저혈압, ㉧ 빈혈, ㉨ 심장판막증, ㉩ 견비통 등이 있어요.

Circulatory diseases include the following : ㉠ stroke, ㉡ arteriosclerosis ㉢ myocardial infarction (MI), ㉣ arrhythmias ㉤ backache, ㉥ hypertension, ㉦ hypotension, ㉧ anemia, ㉨ valvular disease of the heart, ㉩ omodynia.

4) 뇌졸중이 뭐예요? What is a stroke[*Nwaejoljung*]?

뇌졸중이란 뇌혈관이 막히거나 터져서 갑자기 쓰러진 후 마비가 오는 질병이에요.

A stroke happens when blood flow to a part of the brain stops due to congestion or rupture of blood vessels to the brain.

5) 동맥경화가 뭐예요? What is arteriosclerosis[*Dongmaek Gyeonghwa*]?

동맥경화란 동맥이 좁아지는 질병이에요.

Arteriosclerosis is a disease caused by the narrowing of arteries.

6) 심근경색이 뭐예요? What is a myocardial infarction[*Shimgeun Gyeongsaek*]?

심근경색이란 심장 근육의 일부가 죽는 질병이에요.

A myocardial infarction happens when blood flow to the heart is blocked and part of heart muscle dies.

7) 부정맥이 뭐예요? What is an arrhythmia[*Bujeongmaek*]?

부정맥이란 심장이 불규칙하게 뛰는 질병이에요.

An arrhythmia is an irregular heartbeat.

8) 요통이 뭐예요? What is a backache[*Yotong*]?

요통이란 허리에 생기는 통증이에요.

A backache is a pain in the back.

9) 고혈압이 뭐예요? What is hypertension[*Gohyeorap*]?

고혈압이란 혈액이 혈관 벽에 높은 압력을 가하는 질병이에요.

Hypertension is a state in which the blood exerts an increased amount of pressure on the artery wall as it is pumped from the heart.

10) 저혈압이 뭐예요? What is hypotension[*Jeohyerap*]?

저혈압이란 혈액이 혈관 벽에 가하는 압력이 정상보다 낮은 상태를 말해요.

Hypotension is a state in which the blood exerts a decreased amount of pressure on the artery walls as it is pumped from the heart.

11) 빈혈이 뭐예요? What is anemia[*Binhyeol*]?

빈혈이란 혈액 속에 적혈구나 헤모글로빈의 수치가 정상치보다 낮은 상태를 말합니다. 그 결과, 철분이 결핍되거나 체세포로 산소를 운반하는 기능이 저하 됩니다.

Anemia happens when there is a lower than normal number of red blood cells, or hemoglobin, in the blood. This leads to iron deficiency and decreased oxygen transporation to body cells.

12) 심장판막증이 뭐예요? What is a valvular disease of the heart [*Shimjang Panmakjeung*]?

심장판막증이란 심장판막에 이상이 생겨 피가 제멋대로 흐르는 상태를 말해요.

A valvular disease of the heart is the abnormal blood stream caused by the malfunction of the heart valve.

13) 견비통이 뭐예요? What is omodynia[*Gyeonbitong*]?

견비통이란 어깨에서 팔까지 저리고 아픈 질병이에요.

Omodynia is pain or cramping anywhere from the shoulder to the arm.

14) 호흡기가 뭐예요? What are the respiratory organs[*Hoheupgi*]?

① 호흡기란 호흡 작용을 하는 기관이에요.

The respiratory organs are the organs related to breathing.

② 호흡기에는 ㉠ 비강, ㉡ 인두, ㉢ 후두, ㉣ 기관, ㉤ 기관지, ㉥ 허파가 있어요.

Respiratory organs include the ㉠ nasal cavity, ㉡ pharynx, ㉢ larynx, ㉣ trachea, ㉤ bronchus, ㉥ lungs.

15) 신장이 뭐예요? What is a kidney[*Shinjang*]?

① 신장은 콩팥이라고도 해요.

Kidney is called soy bean and red bean[Kongpat].

② 신장은 오줌을 내보내는 곳이에요.

A kidney produces urine.

16) 내분비계가 뭐예요? What is the internal secretion system[*Naebunbigye*]?

① 내분비계란 호르몬을 분비하는 기관을 말해요.

The internal secretion system is composed of all the organ that secretes hormones.

② 호르몬에는 ㉠ 성장 호르몬, ㉡ 여성 호르몬, ㉢ 남성 호르몬 등이 있어요.

The hormones which are secreted include : ㉠ somatotropin (growth hormone), ⓛ female hormone(estrogen), and ⓒ male hormone (testosterone).

17) 알러지(알레르기)가 뭐예요? What is an allergy?

① 알러지는 알레르기라고도 말해요.

An allergy is an hypersensitive reaction to a specific material.

② 알러지(알레르기)는 어떤 음식이나 물질에 대해서만 ㉠ 두드러기, ㉡ 콧물, ㉢ 기침, ㉣ 가려움 ㉤ 상기도 폐색 등이 나타나는 증상이에요.

Allergy symptoms include the following : ㉠ rash, ㉡ runny nose, ㉢ cough, ㉣ itching and ㉤ occlusion of airway.

18) 류마티스가 뭐예요? What is rheumatism?

류마티스란 근육이나 관절에 염증을 일으키는 질병이에요.

Rheumatism is a painful disorder of the joints or connective tissues.

19) 감염이 뭐예요? What is an infection[*Gamyeom*]?

① 감염이란 ㉠ 세균, ㉡ 바이러스, ㉢ 곰팡이 등에 의해 신체가 오염된 경우를 말해요.

Infection is a contamination of the body by ㉠ germs, ㉡ viruses, and ㉢ fungus.

② 감염에는 ㉠ 세균 감염, ㉡ 에이즈 감염, ㉢ 결핵균 감염, ㉣ 요로 감염 등이 있어요.

Infections include ㉠ viral infections, ㉡ AIDS infections, ㉢ Tuberculosis infections, and ㉣ urinary track infections.

20) 혈액 종양이 뭐예요? What is a blood tumor[*Hyeolaek Jongyang*]?

① 혈액 종양이란 혈액에 병이 생기는 거예요.

A blood tumor is a disease in the bloo.

② 혈액 종양에는 ㉠ 백혈병, ㉡ 재생 불량성 빈혈 등이 있어요.

The blood tumor includes ㉠ leukemia and ㉡ aplastic anemia.

3. 유용한 표현 Useful Expressions

1) 내과 치료는 어떻게 해요?

How does the internal medicine department treat the patient?

주로 약물 치료를 해요.

They mainly use medicine.

2) 어떤 증상이 있을 때 내과에 가요?

When should I go to the internal medicine department?

(1) 소화기 내과 Digestive Internal Medicine

① 입 냄새가 심하면 소화기 내과에 가요.

You go to the digestive internal medicine department when you have foul breath.

② 속이 쓰리면 소화기 내과에 가요.

You go to the digestive internal medicine department when you have stomach pain.

③ 식욕이 없으면 소화기 내과에 가요.

You go to the digestive internal medicine department when you have a loss of appetitie.

(2) 순환기 내과 Circulatory Internal Medicine

① 허리가 아프면 순환기 내과에 가요.

You should go to the circulatory internal medicine department when you have a back pain.

㉮ 허리가 끊어질 듯이 아프면 순환기 내과에 가요.

You should go to the circulatory internal medicine department when you have a serious back pain.

㉯ 허리를 펴기 어려우면 순환기 내과에 가요.

You should go to the circulatory internal medicine department when you have difficulty straightening your back.

㉰ 허리를 구부리기 어려우면 순환기 내과에 가요.

You should go to the circulatory internal medicine department when you have difficulty bending your back.

② 자주 어지러우면 순환기 내과에 가요.

You should go to the circulatory internal medicine department if you frequently feel dizzy.

③ 혈압이 높거나 낮으면 순환기 내과에 가요.

You should go to the circulatory internal medicine department if you have high or low blood pressure.

④ 심장이 아프면 순환기 내과에 가요.

You should go to the circulatory internal medicine department if you have a pain in your heart.

⑤ 어깨가 아프면 순환기 내과에 가요.

You should go to the circulatory internal medicine department when you have a pain in your shoulder.

(3) 호흡기 내과 Respiratory Internal Medicine

① 기침이 심하면 호흡기 내과에 가요.

You should go to the respiratory internal medicine department when you have a serious cough.

② 코가 자주 막히면 호흡기 내과에 가요.

You should go to the respiratory internal medicine department when you have frequent nasal congestion.

③ 숨 쉬기가 어려우면 호흡기 내과에 가요.

You should go to the respiratory internal medicine department when you have difficulty breathing.

④ 가슴이 답답하면 호흡기 내과에 가요.

You should go to the respiratory internal medicine department when you feel stuffy chest due to congestion in your lungs.

⑤ 숨이 차면 호흡기 내과에 가요.

You should go to the respiratory internal medicine department if you feel you are panting.

⑥ 가슴이 쿵쿵 뛰면 호흡기 내과에 가요.

You should go to the respiratory internal medicine department if your heart is beating very hard and fast.

(4) 신장 내과 Kidney Internal Medicine

① 몸이 자주 부으면 신장 내과에 가요.

You should go to the kidney internal medicine department if your body is often swollen/edematous.

② 소변을 자주 보면 신장 내과에 가요.

You should go to the kidney internal medicine department if you have to urine too frequently.

③ 소변 볼 때 통증이 있으면 신장 내과에 가요.

You should go to the kidney internal medicine department if you have a pain while urinating.

(5) 내분비계 내과 Internal Secretion

① 몸의 특정 부위가 살이 찌면 내분비계 내과에 가요.

You should go to the internal secretion department if you gain weight only in a specific part of your body.

② 키가 안 크면 내분비계 내과에 가요.

You should go to the internal secretion department when you don't grow up in height.

(6) 알러지(알레르기) 내과 Allergy Internal Medicine

① 두드러기나 자주 나면 알러지(알레르기) 전문병원에 가요.

You should go to the Allergy Clinic if you have rashes very frequently.

② 꽃가루가 날릴 때 심한 기침을 하면 알러지(알레르기) 전문병원에 가요.

You should go to the Allergy Clinic if you get a serious cough every spring.

(7) 류마티스 내과 Rheumatism Internal Medicine

① 손가락, 손목, 팔꿈치가 붓거나 아프면 류마티스 전문병원에

가요.

You should go to the Rheumatism Clinic if your fingers, wrists, or elbows are swollen.

② 무릎, 발목, 발가락이 붓거나 아프면 류마티스 전문병원에 가요.

You should go to the Rheumatism Clinic if your knees, ankles, and toes are swollen or painful.

③ 손발이 차가우면 류마티스 전문병원에 가요.

You should go to the Rheumatism Clinic if your hands and feet often feel cold.

④ 관절이 아프면 류마티스 전문병원에 가요.

You should go to the Rheumatism Clinic if you have a pain in your joints.

⑤ 손발이 저리면 류마티스 전문병원에 가요.

You should go to the Rheumatism Clinic if your hands and feet feel numb.

⑥ 발에 자주 쥐가 나면 류마티스 전문병원에 가요.

You should go to the Rheumatism Clinic if your feet cramp frequently.

(8) 혈액종양 내과 Blood Tumor Internal Medicine

① 코피가 심하게 나면 혈액종양 내과에 가요.

When you have a serious nose blood, you should go to the blood tumor department.

② 목 주위, 겨드랑이, 사타구니 등에 덩어리가 생겨 자라나면 혈액종양 내과에 가요.

When you have scarcomas around your neck, armpits and groin area, you should go to the blood tumor department.

4. 현장 한국어 Korean in Practice

① 입 냄새가 심해요. I have seriously foul breath.

② 속이 쓰려요. I have stomach pain.

③ 자주 구토가 나요. I throw up often.

④ 식욕이 없어요. I have no appetite.

⑤ 자주 어지러워요. I often feel dizzy.

⑥ 혈압이 높아요. I have high blood pressure (hypertension).

⑦ 혈압이 낮아요. I have low blood pressure (hypotension).

⑧ 기침이 심해요. I have a serious cough.

⑨ 코가 자주 막혀요. I have frequent nasal congestion.

⑩ 숨 쉬기가 어려워요. I have difficulty breathing.

⑪ 얼굴이 자주 부어요. My face is frequently swollen.

⑫ 키가 안 커요. I am not growing up in height.

⑬ 두드러기가 자주 나요. I frequently have rashes.

⑭ 소변을 자주 봐요. I am urinating more than usual.

⑮ 피부가 심하게 가려워요. My skin seriously itches.

07

이비인후과
Ear, Nose, Throat(ENT) Department

1. 핵심어 Key Words

① 이비인후과 ENT Department

② 코골이 Snoring

③ 귀울음 Tinnitus

④ 축농증 Sinusitis

⑤ 비염 Rhinitis

⑥ 알레르기 비염 Allergic Rhinitis

⑦ 편도선 Tonsillitis

⑧ 중이염 Otitis Media

⑨ 실어증 Aphasia

⑩ 귓바퀴(심이) Auricle

2. 단어 Words

1) 이비인후과가 뭐예요? What is the ENT department?

이비인후과는 ㉠ 귀, ㉡ 코, ㉢ 목, ㉣ 목구멍, ㉤ 기관, ㉥ 식도의 병을 치료하는 곳이에요.

The ENT department deals with diseases related to the following : ㉠ ear, ㉡ nose, ㉢ throat, ㉣ tonsil, ㉤ trachea, and ㉥ esophagus.

2) 기관이 뭐예요? What is the trachea?

기관이란 숨을 쉴 때 공기를 통과시키는 관이에요.

The trachea is a passageway that air passes through when we breathe.

3) 식도가 뭐예요? What is the esophagus?

식도란 삼킨 음식을 위로 보내는 관이에요.

The esophagus is a passageway that sends food to the stomach.

4) 인후염이 뭐예요? What is a sore throat?

① 인후염이란 인후에 염증이 생긴 것이에요.

A sore throat is caused by an infection in the throat.

② 인후란 목구멍이라고도 해요.

The throat is also called "*Mokgumeong*".

③ 염증이란 몸의 일부가 붓거나 빨갛게 되거나 열이 나거나 아픈 증상이에요.

Symptoms of infection are swelling, reddening, fever, and pain in the body.

5) 코골이가 뭐예요? What is snoring?

① 코골이란 잠을 잘 때 입으로 숨을 쉬면서 소리를 내는 것이에요.
Snoring is a noise created by obstructed air movements that occur during sleep.

② 코콜이가 심하다는 말은 '코를 심하게 곤다'라는 뜻이에요.
'Having serious snoring' means snoring heavily.

6) 축농증이 뭐예요? What is Sinusitis?

① 축농증이란 코에 고름이 있는 거예요.
The Sinusitis is the symptom of having pus in the pleural cavity.

② 고름이란 몸에 염증이 있을 때 생기는 노르스름한 빛의 액체를 말해요.
Pus is a yellow sticky liquid that results from bodily infection.

③ 축농증이 있으면 코가 자주 막히고 콧물이 나와요.
If you have synusitis, you have nasal congestion and a runny nose.

7) 비염이 뭐예요? What is Rhinitis?

① 비염이란 코 안이 붓는 거예요.
The Rhinitis is a inflammation or irritation in the nose.

② 비염이 생기면 맑은 콧물이 흐르고 재채기가 나요.
When you have rhinitis, you may have a runny nose and sneeze often.

8) 중이염이 뭐예요? What is Otitis Media?

① 중이염이란 귀에 고름이 있는 거예요.
Otitis Media is infection or inflammation of the middle ear.

② 중이염이 생기면 귀가 아프고 열이 나요.

If you have Otitis Media, you will have a fever and pain in your ear.

③ 귀에 물이 들어가면 중이염이 생기기 쉬워요.

If water gets into the ear, you are more likely to have otitis media.

9) 고막이 뭐예요? What is the eardrum?

① 고막이란 귓구멍 안쪽에 있는 막이에요.

The eardrum is a tympanic membrane located inside of the ear.

② 고막이 다치면 소리를 들을 수 없어요.

If you hurt your eardrum, you may experience hearing loss.

10) 편도가 뭐예요? What are tonsils?

① 편도란 목구멍 뒤쪽에 있는 작은 덩어리예요.

Tonsils are small masses located in the back of the throat.

② 편도선염은 편도가 붓고 아픈 증상을 보여요.

Symptoms of tonsillitis include swelling and pain in the tonsils.

11) 난청이 뭐예요? What is "hearing-impaired?"

난청이란 소리를 들을 수 없는 상태를 말해요.

Being hearing-impaired means having difficulty hearing.

12) 이명이 뭐예요? What is tinnitus?

① '이명'이란 귀에서 소리가 나는 것이에요.

"Tinnitus" is a ringing sound in the ear.

② '이명'은 '귀울음'이라고도 해요.

"Tinnitus" is also called "ear-ringing".

13) 보청기가 뭐예요? What is a hearing aid?

① 보청기란 소리를 잘 들리게 하는 기구예요.

A hearing aid is a device that helps people with bad hearing hear better.

② 보청기는 귀에 꽂고 다녀요.

A hearing aid is attached to the ear.

③ '할머니, 보청기를 귀에 끼세요'라고 말해요.

You should say, "Ma'am, please put your hearing aid in your ear."

④ '할머니, 보청기를 귀에서 빼세요'라고 말해요.

You should say, "Ma'am, please take out your hearing aid."

14) 만성 축농증이 뭐예요? What is Chronic Empyema?

① '만성'이란 오래된 버릇처럼 오랫동안 아파서 쉽게 낫지 않는 상태예요.

'Chronic' refers to a long term habitual state of disease.

② 만성 축농증이란 축농증이 오래 되었다는 뜻이에요.

Chronic Sinusitis is a long lasted nose disease.

15) 급성이 뭐예요? What is Acute?

① '급성'이란 '만성'과 반대예요.

'Acute' is the opposite of 'chronic.'

② '급성'이란 병이 갑자기 생겨서 빠르게 진행되는 상태를 말해요.

'Acute' is a sudden and very fast progression of a disease.

3. 유용한 표현 Useful Expressions

1) '귀가 어둡다'라는 말의 뜻이 뭐예요?
   What does 'dark in the ear (*Gwiga Eodupda*)' mean?

   ① '귀가 어둡다'라는 말은 소리가 안 들린다는 뜻이에요.

   '*Gwiga Eodupda*' means I can't hear well.

   ② 소리가 완전히 안 들리는 경우에는 '귀가 절벽이다'라고 하기도 해요.

   When someone cannot hear anything, he says, "I have a cliff of an ear".

   ③ '귀가 절벽이다'라는 말은 '세상의 소식을 잘 모른다'는 뜻으로 쓰기도 해요.

   "I have a cliff of an ear" means I don't know what's going on in the world.

2) '코고는 소리가 요란하다'라는 말의 뜻이 뭐예요?
   What does "*Kogoneun Soriga Yoranhada*" mean?

   '코고는 소리가 요란하다'라는 말은 '코고는 소리가 크다'는 뜻이에요.
   "*Kogoneun Soriga Yoranhada*" means you snore very loudly.

3) '헛코골지 말고 어서 일어나라'는 말의 뜻이 뭐예요?
   What does "*Heokko goljimalgo Ireonara*" mean?

   ① '헛코골다'라는 말은 잠을 자지 않으면서도 자는 체 하느라고 거짓으로 코를 곤다는 뜻이에요.

   "*Heokko golda*" means you are pretending to sleep by snoring.

   ② '헛코골지 말고 어서 일어나라'는 말은 '잠이 깼으면 어서 일어나라'는 뜻이에요.

"*Heokko goljimalgo Ireonara*" means "You should get up if you are awake".

4) '눈치가 빠르다'라는 말의 뜻이 뭐예요?
   What does "*Nunchiga Pareuda*" mean?

   ① '눈치가 빠르다'라는 말은 남의 속마음을 빨리 알아챈다는 뜻이
   에요.
   "*Nunchiga Pareuda*" means you can read what people are thinking.

   ② '눈치가 빠르다'라는 말은 순발력이 좋다는 뜻이기도 해요.
   "*Nunchiga Pareuda*" means you have a good instantaneous reaction.

   ③ '순발력이 좋다'라는 말은 어려운 상황을 빠른 시간 안에 잘 극
   복한다는 뜻이에요.
   "*Sunbalyeogi Jotta*" means you can get over a very difficult situation
   in a very short period of time.

5) '눈치코치도 없다'는 말의 뜻이 뭐예요?
   What does "*Nunchi Kochido Eopda*" mean?

   ① '눈치코치도 없다'는 말은 진지한 분위기의 상황에서 아무 것도
   모르는 경우를 말해요.
   "*Nunchi Kochido Eopda*" means you cannot understand a very serious
   situation.

   ② '눈치코치도 없다'는 말은 전혀 다른 말을 하거나 엉뚱한 행동
   을 하는 경우를 말해요.
   "*Nunchi Kochido Eopda*" means you're talking about or doing
   nonsense.

4. 현장 한국어 Korean in Practice

1) 어떤 증상이 있을 때 이비인후과에 가요?

① 귀가 아프면 이비인후과에 가요.

When you have an earache, you should go to the ENT department.

② 코가 아프면 이비인후과에 가요.

When you have a problem with your nose, you should go to the ENT department.

③ 목이 아프면 이비인후과에 가요.

When you have a sore throat, you should go to the ENT department.

④ 귀가 잘 안 들리면 이비인후과에 가요.

If you can't hear well, you should go to the ENT department.

⑤ 기침을 많이 하면 이비인후과에 가요.

When you have a serious cough, you should go to the ENT department.

⑥ 귀에서 소리가 나면 이비인후과에 가요.

If you have a ringing sound in your ear, you should go to the ENT department.

⑦ 코를 심하게 골면 이비인후과에 가요.

If you snore heavily, you should go to the ENT department.

⑧ 편도가 부으면 이비인후과에 가요.

If you have swollen tonsils, you should go to the ENT department.

2) 아픈 증상을 말할 때 이렇게 하세요.

You can explain your symptoms as follows.

코 NOSE

① 코가 막혔어요. I have nasal congestion.

② 콧속이 아파요. I have a pain in my nostrils.

③ 콧속이 헐었어요 I have canker sores in my nose.

④ 코가 말라요. My nostril gets dry.

⑤ 코피가 나요. I have a nose bleed.

⑥ 콧물이 나요. I have a runny nose.

⑦ 맑은 콧물이 흘러요. I have clear nose drippings.

⑧ 노란 콧물이 흘러요. I have yellow nose drippings.

⑨ 숨을 쉴 수가 없어요. I can't breathe.

⑩ 냄새를 맡을 수 없어요. I can't smell.

귀 EAR

① 귀에 물이 들어갔어요. I have water in my ear.

② 귀가 아파요. I have an earache.

③ 귓속이 아파요. I have pain inside my ear.

④ 귀에서 고름이 나요. The pus oozes out of my ear.

⑤ 귀가 잘 안 들려요. I can't hear well.

⑥ 귀가 먹었어요. I'm deaf.

⑦ 귀가 간지러워요. My ear is itchy.

⑧ 귀에서 소리가 나요. There is a ringing sound in my ear.

⑨ 귀가 멍멍해요. I'm just deafened.

⑩ 귀지가 찼어요. My ear is full of earwax.

목구멍 THROAT

① 목구멍이 아파요. I have a sore throat.

② 목이 자주 잠겨요. My voice gets hoarse very often.

③ 목이 쉬었어요. My voice is hoarse.

④ 편도가 부었어요. My tonsils are swollen.

⑤ 목이 따끔거려요. My throat stings.

⑥ 목이 칼칼해요. I have a dry throat.

⑦ 목이 간질거려요. My throat is itchy.

⑧ 목소리가 안 나와요. I lost my voice.

⑨ 목이 부었어요. My throat is swollen.

⑩ 침을 삼킬 수가 없어요. I can't swallow my spit.

08 비뇨기과
Urology Department

1. 핵심어 Key Words

① 비뇨기과 Department of Urology

② 신장 Kidney

③ 방광 Bladder

④ 빈뇨 Pollakiuria

⑤ 요로 Urinary Tract

⑥ 결석 Lithiasis (stone)

2. 단어 Words

1) 비뇨기과가 뭐예요? What is *Binyogigwa* (Urology Department)?

① 비뇨기과는 비뇨기에 관한 병을 치료하는 곳이에요.

The urology department deals with diseases related to the urinary system.

② 비뇨기란 오줌을 만들어 배설하는 기관이에요.

The urinary system consists of organs that are involved in the creation of urine.

③ 비뇨기에는 신장, 방광, 요도가 있어요.

The urinary system includes the kidneys, the bladder, and the urinary tract.

2) 배설기관이 뭐예요? What is *Baeseolgigwan* (Excretory organs)?

① 배설이란 몸 안의 찌꺼기를 몸 밖으로 내보내는 활동을 말해요.

Excretion is the activity of releasing wastes from the body.

② 배설되는 몸 안의 찌꺼기는 오줌과 땀이에요.

The released wastes of the body are urine and sweat.

③ 배설기관이란 몸 안의 찌꺼기를 몸 밖으로 내보내는 곳이에요.

The excretory organs are used to release the wastes of the body.

④ 배설기관에는 콩팥과 땀샘이 있어요.

The excretory organs include the kidneys and perspiratory glands.

3) 부종이 뭐예요? What is *Bujong* (edema)?

부종이란 몸이 붓는 증상이에요.

Edema is a symptom, defined as swelling in the body.

4) 신장이 뭐예요? What is *Shinjang* (kidney)?

① 신장이란 오줌을 만드는 곳이에요.

A kidney is an organ that makes urine.

② 신장에서는 혈액 속의 노폐물과 수분을 걸러요.

Kidneys filter off wastes and excess water from the blood.

③ 신장에서 걸러진 오줌은 방광 속에 괴어 있다가 몸 밖으로 나가요.

The urine that is produced by the kidneys stay in the bladder before it is released out of the body.

5) 방광이 뭐예요? What is *Banggwang* (Bladder)?

① 방광이란 오줌을 저장했다가 배출시키는 곳이에요.

The blader is an organ that the urine stays in before it is released from the body.

② 방광은 다른 말로 '오줌통'이라고도 해요.

The bladder is also called "*Ojumtong*" (urine barrel).

6) 혈액이 뭐예요? What is *Hyeolaek* (blood)?

혈액이란 '피'와 같은 말이에요.

"*Hyeolaek*" means "Blood (*pi*)"

7) 노폐물이 뭐예요? What is *Nopyemul* (wastes)?

① 노폐물이란 '필요 없는 것'이란 뜻이에요.

Wastes mean things unnecessary to the body.

② 노폐물이란 '쓸모없는 것'이란 뜻이에요.

Wastes mean things that are not useful for the body.

8) 수분이 뭐예요? What is *Subun* (moisture)?

① 수분이란 '물기'라는 뜻이에요.

Moisture is wetness.

② 물기란 '축축한 물의 기운'이라는 뜻이에요.

Wetness is the sensation created by the presence of water.

9) 빈뇨가 뭐예요? What is *Binnyo* (frequent urination)?

① 빈뇨란 오줌을 자주 보는 증세를 말해요.

Frequent urination means urinating too often.

② 하루에 소변을 10번 이상 보면 '빈뇨'라고 해요.

The patient with frequent urination urinates over 10 times per day.

10) 요실금이 뭐예요? What is *Yoshilgeum* (incontinent of urine)?

① 요실금이란 소변이 저절로 나오는 것이에요.

Incontinent of urine is the inability to retain urine, resulting in unintentional urination.

② 요실금이 있으면 소변을 참을 수 없어요.

If the patient is incontinent of urine, he or she cannot retain urine.

11) 요도가 뭐예요? What is *Yodo* (Urethra)?

① 요도란 '요로'라고도 해요.

The urethra is part of the urinary tract.

② 요로란 오줌을 밖으로 배출하기 위한 관이에요.

The urinary tract is the passageway through which urine is released.

12) 결석이 뭐예요? What is *Gyeolseok* (lithiasis)?

① 결석이란 몸 안에 생기는 돌이에요.

Lithiasis is a very small stone that forms in the body.

② 신장에 돌이 생기면 '신장결석'이라고 해요.

If the stones are found in the kidneys, they are called kidney stones.

13) 콩팥이 뭐예요? What is *Kongpat* (kidney)?

① 콩팥이란 '신장'이라고도 해요.

'*Kongpat*' is kidney.

② 콩팥이란 콩 모양의 배설기관을 말해요.

Kindneys are excretory organs that are shaped like beans.

14) 만성신장염이 뭐예요?

What is *Manseong Shinjangyeom* (Chronic nephritis)?

① 만성이란 버릇이 되다시피 하여 쉽게 고쳐지지 않는 상태를 말해요.

A chronic disease is a habituated, incurable disease.

② 만성신장염이란 만성콩팥염이라고도 해요.

Chronic nephritis is also called chronic inflammation of the kidney.

③ 만성신장염은 병이 나았다 더했다 하면서 1년 이상 지속되는 염증을 말해요. Chronic nephritis is the continual inflammation of the kidney for more than one year.

15) 급성신장염이 뭐예요?

What is *Keupseong Shinjangyeom* (acute nephritis)?

① 급성이란 병의 증세가 갑자기 나타나는 상태를 말해요.

An acute disease is a disease that happens all of a sudden.

② 급성신장염이란 신장에 염증이 생긴 후 6개월까지를 말해요.

In case of acute nephritis, there is sudden inflammation of the kidney that does not last for more than 6 months.

16) 혈뇨가 뭐예요? What is *Hyeolnyo* (Hematuria)?

혈뇨란 소변에 피가 섞여 나오는 것을 말해요.

Hematuria is blood in the urine.

17) 요로감염이 뭐예요? What is *Yoro Gamyeom* (Urinary Tract Infection)?

요로감염이란 오줌이 지나가는 관을 통해 병에 걸린 상태를 말해요.

A urinary tract infection is an infection in the tract that the urine passes through.

18) 방광염이 뭐예요? What is *Banggwangyeom* (Cystitis)?

방광염이란 방광에 염증이 생긴 병이에요.

Cystitis is inflammation of the bladder.

3. 유용한 표현 Useful Expressions

1) 어떤 증상이 있을 때 비뇨기과에 가요?

When do you go to the Urology Department?

① 몸이 자주 부으면 비뇨기과에 가요.

You should go to the urology department when you have frequent edema.

② 신장 부분이 심하게 아프면 비뇨기과에 가요.

You should go to the urology department when you have a serious pain in the kidney area.

③ 오줌이 자주 마려우면 비뇨기과에 가요.

You should go to the urology department when you feel an urge to urinate so often.

④ 오줌에 피가 섞여 나오면 비뇨기과에 가요.

You should go to the urology department when you have blood in the urine.

⑤ 소변 볼 때 통증이 있으면 비뇨기과에 가요.

You should go to the urology department when you have a pain in urination.

⑥ 소변을 참을 수 없으면 비뇨기과에 가요.

You should go to the urology department when you can't retain your urine.

⑦ 소변이 저절로 나오면 비뇨기과에 가요.

You should go to the urology department when you have unintentional urination.

⑧ 옆구리와 하복부가 심하게 아프면 비뇨기과에 가요.

You should go to the urology department when you have an acute pain in the side and lower abdomen.

가) '오줌이 탁히디'라는 밀의 뜻이 뭐예요?

What does "*Ojumi Takada*(You have thick urination)"?

① '오줌이 탁하다'라는 말은 '오줌이 맑다'의 반대말이에요.

"Thick urination" is the opposite of "clear urine".

② 오줌에 쌀뜨물같이 하얀 것이 섞여 있으면 '오줌이 탁하다'고

해요.

When the urine contains white water like rice-washing water, we call it the thick urine.

③ '오줌이 탁하다'라는 말은 '오줌이 불투명하다'라는 말과 같아요.

Thick urine is the same with milky urine.

또는 오줌이 투명하지 못하다고 말하기도 해요.

It also means the urine is not transparent.

④ 건강한 오줌은 '투명'한 액체의 형태예요.

Healthy urine is in the form of transparent liquid.

⑤ '오줌이 탁하다.' 또는 '소변이 탁하다.'라고 말해요.

We say "The piss is thick," or "The urine is milky."

⑥ 오줌이 탁하면 배설기관에 병이 있는 거예요.

When the urine is milky, it may mean that you have a disease in the excretory organ.

4) '오줌소태'가 뭐예요? What is *Ojum Sotae*(Pollakiuria)?

'오줌소태'라는 말은 오줌이 자주 마려운 병이라는 뜻이에요.

The pollakiuria is a disease of frequent feeling of urination.

5) '요실금 패드'가 뭐예요? What is *Yoshilgeum*(irretention of urine) Pad?

① '요실금 패드'란 오줌이 저절로 나오는 사람들이 사용하는 기저귀예요.

"*Yoshilgeum* Pad" is a diaper for the people who have unintentional urination.

② 기저귀란 대변과 소변을 받아내는 천이예요.

A diaper is a piece of cloth to take stools and urination.

③ 패드는 천 대신 흡수성이 강한 물질로 만든 화학 기저귀예요.

A pad is a chemical diaper made of a strong absorbent materials.

4. 현장 한국어 Korean in Practice

1) 아픈 증상을 말할 때 이렇게 하세요.

You can talk about your symptoms as follows ;

① 몸이 자주 부어요.

My body swells very often.

② 신장 부분(옆구리와 하복부)이 심하게 아파요.

I have acute pains in my side and lower abdomen area, where the kidneys are located.

③ 아랫배가 아파요.

I have a pain in the lower abdominal area.

① 오줌이 자주 마려워요.

I feel frequent urges to urinate.

② 오줌에 피가 섞여 나와요.

My urine contains blood.

③ 소변 볼 때 통증이 심해요.

I have a pain in urination.

④ 소변을 참을 수 없어요.

I can't retain my urination.

⑤ 소변이 저절로 나와요.

I have unintentional urination.

⑥ 소변에 피가 섞여 나와요.

I have bloody urination.

⑦ 소변보기가 힘들어요.

I have difficulty in urination.

⑧ 오줌 눌 때 배가 몹시 아파요.

I have an acute stomachache in urination.

⑨ 오줌이 자주 마렵고 탁해요.

I feel an urge to urinate so often, and it's thick.

09 안과
Ophthalmology Department

1. 핵심어 Key Words

1) 안과 Ophthalmology

2) 눈 Eye

3) 시력 Eyesight

4) 백내장 Cataract

5) 근시 Myopia/ Near-sightedness

6) 원시 Hypermetropia/ Farsightedness

7) 난시 Astigmatism/ Distorted vision

8) 시력 검사표 Eye Test Chart

9) 눈곱 Discharge from the Eyes

10) 안구 건조증 Xerophthalmia

11) 라식 LASIK(Laser Assisted In-Situ Keratomileusis)

12) 라섹 LASEK(Laser Assisted Sb-Epithelial Keratectomy)

13) 안내 렌즈 삽입술 ICL(Implantable Contact Lens Implant Surgery)

14) 안압 Intraocular Pressure

15) 각막 Cornea

16) 초점 Focus

17) 각막염 Coreitis

18) 결막염 Conjunctivitis

19) 백내장 Cataract

20) 녹내장 Glaucoma

21) 다래끼 Sty

22) 각막 Cornea

23) 홍채 Iris

24) 동공 Pupil

2. 단어 Words

1) 눈을 보세요. Look at the eye.

▸ 눈의 구조
The structure of an eye
결막 Conjunctiva
상안검 Upper eyelid
각막 Cornea
하안검 Lower eyelid
수정체 crystalline lens
초자체 Hyaline body
망막 Retina
상직근 Superial rectus
하직근 Inferior rectus
시속 Optic nerve

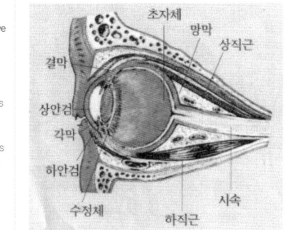

⟨눈의 구조⟩ The structure of an eye

2) 안과가 뭐예요? What is *Angwa* (the department of ophthalmology)?

① 안과는 눈과 관련된 병을 치료하는 곳이에요.

The ophthalmology department deals with the diseases related with eyes.

② 눈은 빛의 자극을 받아 물체를 볼 수 있는 기관이에요.

An eye is an organ to see things with help of light.

3) 안과의가 뭐예요? Who is an *Angwaeui* (Ophthalmologist)?

안과의란 눈과 관련된 병을 치료하는 의사 선생님이에요.

An ophthalmologist is a doctor who deals with the diseases in an eye.

4) 눈곱이 뭐예요? What is *Nunkop* (Discharges from an eye)?

① 눈곱이란 눈에서 나오는 액체예요.

Nunkop is a kind of liquid discharged from an eye.

② 눈곱은 진득진득한 물같이 나왔다가 마르면 딱딱하게 굳어요.

It is at first like sticky liquid, and dries hard later.

5) 시력 검사표가 뭐예요? What is *Shyryeok Geomsa Pyo* (Eye test chart)?

① 시력이란 물체를 알아볼 수 있는 눈의 능력을 뜻해요.

Shiryeok(Eyesight) is an ability of the eye to recognize things.

② 시력 검사란 눈의 능력이 좋은지 나쁜지를 알아보는 거예요.

Shiryeok Geomsa(Eye test) is to check the eyesight.

③ 시력 검사표란 눈의 능력을 알아보기 위해 무언가 써 놓은 판이
에요.

An eye test chart is a plate, on which letters and pictures are
printed to check the eyesight.

④ 시력검사표도 있고 시력검사판도 있어요.

The chart is a table type or a board type.

6) 라식 수술이 뭐예요?

What is *LASIK* (Laser Assisted In-Situ Keratomileusis)?

① 라식 수술이란 시력을 교정하는 수술이에요.

LASIK is a kind of operation to correct the eyesight.

② 라식 수술을 받으면 안경을 쓰지 않아도 잘 볼 수 있어요.

The LASIK operation helps you see well without glasses.

7) 충혈이 뭐예요? What is *Choonghyeol* (blood-shot eyes)?

① 충혈이란 눈자위가 빨갛게 변한 상태를 말해요.

Choonghyeol is a blood shot in the white part of the eyeball.

② 눈자위란 눈알의 언저리를 말해요.

Nunjawee is outer part of the eyeball.

8) 백내장이 뭐예요? What is *Baek Nae Jang* (Cataract)?

백내장이란 눈의 수정체가 회백색으로 흐려져 시력이 떨어지는 병이에요.

The Cataract is a disease by which the crystalline lens turns grey and reduces the eyesight.

9) 녹내장이 뭐예요? What is *Nok Nae Jang* (Glaucoma)?

① 녹내장이란 안구의 압력이 높아져서 잘 못 보는 병이에요.

The Glaucoma is a disease that reduces the eyesight due to increased pressure in the eyeball.

② 안구란 '눈알'을 전문적으로 이르는 말이에요.

Angu means "the eyeball".

10) 근시가 뭐예요? What is *Geunshi* (Myopia)?

① 근시란 가까운 데 있는 것은 잘 보는데 멀리 있는 것은 잘 못
보는 눈을 말해요.

The person with Myopia(Near-sightedness) can see the things near,
but cannot see the things in the distance.

② 근시는 오목렌즈 안경을 써야 해요.

The person with myopia should wear the concave lens-glasses.

11) 원시가 뭐예요? What is *Wonshi* (Hypermetropia)?

① 원시란 가까이에 있는 물체를 잘 못 보는 눈을 말해요.

The person with hypermetropia cannot see the things near.

② 원시는 볼록렌즈 안경을 써야 해요.

The person with hypermetropia should wear bull's-eye glasses.

12) 난시가 뭐예요? What is *Nanshi* (astigmatism)?

난시란 물체를 명확하게 볼 수 없는 눈을 말해요.

The person with astigmatism cannot see things clearly.

13) 안구건조증이 뭐예요? What is *Angu Geonjo Jeung* (Xerophthalmia)?

안구건조증이란 눈알이 눈물에 젖지 않고 하얀 은빛을 나타내는 병
이에요.

The Xerophthalmia is a disease, by which the eyeballs get dry and whitened.

14) 망막 검사가 뭐예요? What is *Mangmak Geomsa* (Retina test)?

① 망막이란 눈알의 가장 안쪽에 있어요.

The retina is located in the deepest part of an eyeball.

② 수정체를 지나온 빛은 망막에 상을 맺어요.

The light puts an image after passing through the pupil.

③ 망막 검사는 망막에 병이 있는지 조사하는 거예요.

The retina test is to check if the retina has any kind of disease.

15) 시력이 뭐예요? What is *Shiryeok* (eyesight)?

시력이란 물체를 인식하는 눈의 능력을 뜻해요.

The eyesight is the ability of an eye to recognize a thing.

16) 시력 검사가 뭐예요? What is *Shiryeok Geomsa* (eye test)?

시력 검사란 눈의 능력이 어느 정도인지를 조사하는 거예요.

The eye test checks the ability of an eye to recognize a thing.

17) 시력 교정이 뭐예요? What is *Shiryeok Gyojeong* (eyesight correction)?

① 시력 교정이란 눈에 안경이나 렌즈를 껴서 시력을 얻는 거예요.

The eyesight correction is to retain a normal eyesight by wearing glasses or lenses.

② 교정시력이란 안경을 낀 상태의 눈의 능력을 말해요.

The corrected eyesight is the ability of the eyes with glasses.

18) 각막이 뭐예요? What is *Gakmak* (Comea)?

① 각막이란 눈알의 앞쪽에 약간 볼록하게 나와 있는 투명한 막이
에요.

The comea is a transparent membrane in the front side of the eyeball.

② 빛은 각막을 통해 눈으로 들어가요.

The light goes into the eyes through the comea.

19) 각막 혼탁이 뭐예요? What is *Gakmak Hontak* (Corneal opacity)?

각막 혼탁이란 각막이 흐려지는 현상이에요.

The Corneal opacity is a symptom that the comea gets opaque.

20) 안경 도수가 뭐예요? What is *Angyeong Dosu* (Lens prescriptions)?

① 안경은 눈에 쓰는 물건이에요.

Glasses are a device for the weak eyesight.

② 안경 도수란 안경의 초점거리를 말해요.

The lens prescriptions describes the focal distance of glasses.

21) 동공이 뭐예요? What is *Donggong* (Pupils)?

동공이란 눈동자와 같은 말이에요.

The pupils are the eyeballs.

22) 후유증이 뭐예요? What is *Huyujeung* (Sequels)?

① 후유증이란 수술을 하거나 약을 먹은 후에 나타나는 부작용을
말해요.

The sequels are a side effect after an operation or medication.

② 부작용이란 원래 일어나야 할 일이 아닌 나쁜 일이 일어나는 상태를 말해요.

The side effect is an undesirable result of a treatment.

23) 재수술이 뭐예요? What is *Jaesusul* (Re-operation)?

재수술이란 수술을 한 후에 결과가 나빠서 다시 수술하는 것을 말해요.

Re-operation is performing an operation again due to the undesirable result of the first operation.

24) 결막염이 뭐예요? What is *Gyeolmakyeom* (Conjunctivitis)?

① 결막염이란 결막에 생기는 염증이에요.

The conjunctivitis is an inflammation in the conjunctiva.

② 결막염이 생기면 눈이 붓고, 충혈 되고 눈곱이 많이 껴요.

The conjunctivitis causes swelling, blood-shot and much discharge in the eye.

25) 다래끼가 뭐예요? What is *Daraeki* (Sty)?

① 다래끼란 눈시울이 빨갛게 붓고 곪아서 생기는 부스럼이에요.

The sty is an abscess in the eyelid with red swelling and infection.

② 눈시울이란 눈언저리의 속눈썹이 난 곳이에요.

The eyelid is the place where the eyelashes grow.

③ 부스럼이란 피부에 나는 종기를 말해요.

The abscess is a kind of sore on the skin.

④ 종기란 피부가 곪으면서 생기는 흔적을 말해요.

The sore is a trace of infection on the skin.

26) 눈물샘이 뭐예요? What is *Nunmulsaem* (lachrymal gland)?

① 눈물샘이란 눈물을 내보내는 곳이에요.

The lachrymal gland is a tract to transfer tears.

② 눈물샘은 눈알이 박혀 움푹 들어간 곳의 바깥 위쪽 구석에 있어요.

The lachrymal gland is located upper outer corner of the eyes.

27) 홍채가 뭐예요? What is *Hongchae* (iris)?

① 홍채란 각막과 수정체 사이에 있는 둥근 모양의 얇은 막이에요.

The iris is a thin round membrane located between the cornea and
the crystalline lens.

② 홍채는 눈에 들어오는 빛의 양을 조절해요.

The iris controls the amount of the light coming into the eye.

3. 유용한 표현 Useful Expressions

1) 어떤 증상이 있을 때 안과에 가요?

When do you go to the ophthalmology department?

① 눈이 아프면 안과에 가요. You should go to the ophthalmology
department when you have a sore eye.

② 눈이 많이 따끔거리면 안과에 가요. You should go to the
ophthalmology department when your eye stings.

③ 눈곱이 많이 끼면 안과에 가요. You should go to the ophthalmology
department when you have a lot of discharges in the eye.

④ 눈이 자주 충혈 되면 안과에 가요. You should go to the ophthal-mology department when you frequently have blood-shot in the eye.

⑤ 백내장 수술하려면 안과에 가요. You should go to the ophthalmology department when you want to have a cataract operation.

⑥ 라식 수술하려면 안과에 가요. You should go to the ophthalmology department when you want to have the LASIK operation.

⑦ 라섹 수술하려면 안과에 가요. You should go to the ophthalmology department when you want to have LASEK operation.

⑧ 시력 교정 수술하려면 안과에 가요. You should go to the ophthalmology department when you want to correct the eyesight.

⑨ 안구건조증이 심하면 안과에 가요. You should go to the ophthal-mology department when you have severe ophthalmoxerosis.

⑩ 결막염이 있으면 안과에 가요. You should go to the ophthalmology department when you have conjunctivitis.

⑪ 다래끼가 심하면 안과에 가요. You should go to the ophthalmology department when you have serious sty.

⑫ 녹내장 수술하려면 안과에 가요. You should go to the ophthalmology department when you want to have glaucoma operation.

⑬ 시력이 많이 떨어지면 안과에 가요. You should go to the ophthalmology department when you lose seriously lose your eyesight.

⑭ 눈물샘이 막히면 안과에 가요. You should go to the ophthalmology department when your lachrymal gland is blocked.

⑮ 눈물이 자주 나오면 안과에 가요. You should go to the ophthal-mology department when you shed a lot of tears.

2) '눈곱이 끼다'라는 말의 뜻이 뭐예요?

What is *Nunkop Kida* (have discharge in the eye)?

① '눈곱이 끼다'라는 말은 눈곱이 말라붙어 있는 상태를 말해요.

"You have some sleep in the eye." means that you have dried mucus in the corner of the eye.

② 눈곱이 끼어 있으면 보기 싫으니까 눈곱을 떼는 것이 좋아요.

It doesn't look good when you have mucus in the eye, so your should get rid of it.

③ '눈곱이 끼다' 대신에 '눈곱이 나온다'고도 말해요.

"You have some sleep in the eye" is the same with "The mucus is coming out of your eye."

3) '눈곱만큼'이 뭐예요? What is *Nunkopmankeum* (the amount of eye mucus)?

① '눈곱만큼'이라는 말은 '양이 아주 적다'는 뜻이에요.

"An amount of eye mucus" means "very little".

② 나는 이 집에 눈곱만큼의 미련도 없다. I don't have even an amount of eye mucus of feelings left for this house.

③ 라면이 눈곱만큼 밖에 없어서 줄 수 없다. I have only an amount of eye mucus of ramyeon, and I can't share it with you.

4. 현장 한국어 Korean in Practice

1) 아픈 증상을 말할 때 이렇게 하세요.

You can talk about your symptoms as follows.

① 눈이 많이 아파요. I have much pain in the eye.

② 눈이 많이 따끔거려요. My eye stings so much.

③ 눈곱이 자주 껴요. I often have discharges in the eye.

④ 눈이 자주 충혈 돼요. I often have a blood-shot eye.

⑤ 백내장 수술하러 왔어요. I came here for a cataract operation.

⑥ 라식 수술하러 왔어요. I came here for LASIK operation.

⑦ 라섹 수술하러 왔어요. I came here for LASEK operation.

⑧ 시력 교정 수술하러 왔어요. I came here for eyesight correction operation.

⑨ 안구건조증이 심해요. I have a severe ophthalmoxerosis.

⑩ 결막염이 있어요. I have conjunctivitis.

⑪ 다래끼가 심해요. I have a severe sty.

⑫ 녹내장 수술하러 왔어요. I came here to a have glaucoma operation.

⑬ 시력이 많이 떨어졌어요. My eyesight has seriously reduced.

⑭ 눈물샘이 막혔어요. My lachrymal gland is blocked.

⑮ 눈이 시려요. I have a sore eye.

⑯ 눈에 이물질이 들어간 것 같아요. I feel a foreign body in the eye.

⑰ 눈이 건조해요. My eyes are dry.

⑱ 눈이 빨개요. My eyes are red.

⑲ 눈이 붓고 간지러워요. My eyelids are swollen and itching.

⑳ 눈알이 가려워요. My eyeballs are itching.

㉑ 눈이 침침해요. I have blear eyes.

㉒ 눈이 잘 안 보여요. I can't see well.

㉓ 물체가 이중으로 보여요. I have a double vision.

㉔ 글씨가 잘 보이지 않아요. I can't see the words well.

2) '눈'과 관련된 말이에요. These are some expressions related with 'eyes'.

① ㉠ 눈을 뜨다. → 눈을 뜨세요. Open your eyes.

　㉡ 눈을 감다. → 눈을 감으세요. Close your eyes.

② ㉠ 눈이 맑다. → 눈이 맑아요. I have clear eyes.

　㉡ 눈이 흐리다. → 눈이 흐려요. I have dim eyes.

③ ㉠ 눈이 좋다. → 눈이 좋아요. I have a good eyesight.

　㉡ 눈이 나쁘다. → 눈이 나빠요. I have a bad eyesight.

④ ㉠ 눈이 밝다. → 눈이 밝아요. I have a keen eyesight.

　㉡ 눈이 어둡다. → 눈이 어두워요. I can't see well.

⑤ 눈이 맞다. → ㉠ 당신 눈이 맞아요.(당신이 옳아요.) You have an
　　　　　　　　　eye for it.(You're right.)

　　　　　　　　→ ㉡ 제 동생이 영화배우와 눈이 맞았어요.
　　　　　　　　　　(제 동생이 영화배우와 사랑에 빠졌어요.) My
　　　　　　　　　　brother eloped with a movie star. (My brother
　　　　　　　　　　fell in love with a movie star.)

⑥ 눈이 정확하다. → 눈이 정확해요. You have an eye for it.

⑦ ㉠ 눈이 초롱초롱하다. → 눈이 초롱초롱해요. Your eyes are shining
　brightly.

　㉡ 눈이 흐리멍텅하다. → 눈이 흐리멍텅해요. You have a glassy
　look.

⑧ ㉠ 눈을 부라리다. → 형이 저에게 눈을 부라렸어요. My elder
　brother glared at me.

　㉡ 눈을 내려 깔다. → 눈을 내려 깔고 앉아 있었어요. He was
　sitting dropping his eyes.

⑨ ㉠ 눈을 치뜨다. → 눈을 치떴어요. He lifted up his eyes.

ⓛ 눈을 내려뜨다. → 눈을 내려떴어요. He lowered his eyes.

⑩ 의심하는 눈으로 보다. → 의심하는 눈으로 보았어요. He gave a suspicious glance.

⑪ 부러워하는 눈으로 바라보다. → 부러워하는 눈으로 바라보았어요. He looked at it with envious eyes.

⑫ 다른 사람의 눈을 의식하다. → 다른 사람의 눈을 의식했어요. He was conscious of others' look.

⑬ 눈이 무섭다. → ㉠ 눈이 무서워요. His eyes are scary.

  → ㉡ 다른 사람의 눈을 무서워해요. He is afraid of other's look.

피부과
Dermatology Department

1. 핵심어 Key Words

1) 피부 Skin

2) 피부과 Department of Dermatology

3) 화장독 Makeup Poison

4) 건성 Arid

5) 지성 Oily

6) 주름 Wrinkle

7) 여드름 Pimples

8) 점 Spot/Birthmark

9) 기미 Melasma

10) 주근깨 Freckles

11) 흉터 Scar

12) 모낭 Hairfollicle

13) 땀샘 Perspiratory Gland

14) 사마귀 Wart/ Mole

15) 수포 Blister

16) 무좀 Athlete's Foot

17) 색소침착 Pigmentation

18) 딱지 Scab

19) 자외선 Ultraviolet Ray

20) 두드러기 Rash

21) 긁은 상처 Scratch

22) 아토피 피부염 An Atopic Dermatitis

23) 연고 Ointment

24) 박피 Decortication

25) 레이저 치료 Laser Therapy

26) 켈로이드 Keloid

27) 안면 홍조 Facial Flushing

28) 모공 축소 Pores Minimizing

2. 단어 Words

1) 피부를 보세요. Look at the skin.

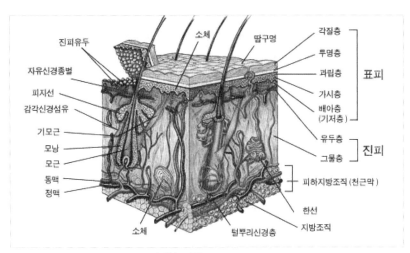

〈피부 조직〉 Human skin

2) 피부가 뭐예요? What is *Pibu* (skin)?

① 피부는 '살갗'이라고도 해요.

The skin is referred to as 'surface skin.'

② 피부는 우리 몸의 가장 겉에 있는 표면이에요.

The skin is the most exterior surface of our body.

③ 피부는 우리 몸의 근육들과 기관을 보호하는 조직이에요.

The skin protects the muscles and organs in the body.

④ 피부는 병원균으로부터 우리 몸을 보호하는 역할을 해요.

The skin protects our body from disease-causing germs.

3) 피부과가 뭐예요? What is *Pibugwa* (Dermatology department)?

피부과는 피부의 질병을 치료하는 의학의 한 분야예요.

The department of dermatology is a part of medicine to treat the skin diseases.

4) 여드름이 뭐예요? What is *Yeodeureum* (Pimples)?

① 여드름이란 주로 얼굴에 나는 종기예요.

Pimples are the rashes on the face.

② 여드름은 검붉은 색으로 오톨도톨하게 나요.

Pimples are in the shape of black and red bumps on the face.

③ 여드름은 털구멍이 막혀서 생겨요.

Pimples are caused by the blocking of pores.

④ 여드름은 등이나 팔에 나기도 해요.

You can have pimples on the arms and back.

5) 화장독이 뭐예요? What is *Hwajangdok* (Makeup poison)?

① 화장독이란 화장품 때문에 생기는 부작용이에요.

The makeup poison is the side effects caused by makeup.

② 화장독은 화장품이 피부에 맞지 않기 때문에 생겨요.

The makeup poison is due to the maladjustment of makeup to skin.

③ 화장독이 생기면 피부가 벌게져요.

The makeup poison makes skin flushed.

6) 기미가 뭐예요? What is *Gimi* (Melasma)?

① 기미는 얼굴에 끼는 검은색 점이에요.

The melasma is a black spot on the face.

② 임신을 하면 얼굴에 기미가 껴요.

When a woman gets pregnant, she has the melasma.

③ 마음고생이 심하면 얼굴에 기미가 껴요.

When a person has deep agony, he/she will have the melasma.

7) 제모가 뭐예요? What is *Jemo* (Hair removing)?

① 제모는 털을 없애는 것이에요.

Jemo means removing hair in the body.

② 한국 여성들은 ㉠ 얼굴의 털, ㉡ 겨드랑이의 털, ㉢ 다리의 털을 깎거나 없애요. Korean women usually shave or remove the hair in the ㉠ face, ㉡ armpit, and ㉢ legs.

8) 아토피가 뭐예요? What is atopy?

① 아토피는 우리 몸에 나타나는 알레르기 반응이에요.

Atopy is one of the allergic reactions of our body.

② 주로 아토피성 피부염이 많아요.

People mainly have atopic dermatitis.

③ 아토피성 피부염은 팔꿈치나 오금의 피부가 두꺼워지면서 까칠까칠해지고 몹시 가려워요.

Atopic dermatitis patients have the skin on the elbows or the groin area get thick, rough and itching.

9) 액취증이 뭐예요? What is *Akchwijeung* (Bromhidrosis)?

① 액취증이란 겨드랑이 냄새 또는 암내라고도 해요.

Bromhidrosis is the severe armpit odor.

② 액취증은 땀이 원인이에요.

Bromhidrosis is caused by sweat.

③ 액취증은 겨드랑이의 땀이 암내를 풍기는 병이에요.

Bromhidrosis is a disease of emitting armpit odor.

10) 흉터가 뭐예요? What is *Hyungteo* (scar)?

흉터란 상처가 아문 후 남은 자국이에요.

A scar is a trace of an injury after getting healed.

11) 안면 홍조가 뭐예요? What is *Anmyeon Hongjo* (facial flushing)?

① 안면 홍조란 얼굴이 붉어진 상태가 오래 지속되는 증상이에요.

Facial flushing is a symptom of a long period of red face.

② 안면 홍조는 사소한 자극에 쉽게 얼굴이 붉어지는 증상이에요.

Facial flushing is a symptom of a face getting red by a trifling stimulus.

③ 안면 홍조는 갑자기 따뜻한 실내에 들어왔을 때 얼굴이 붉어지는 증상이에요. Facial flushing is a symptom of a face getting red after coming in a warm room.

④ 안면 홍조는 술을 마실 때, 만성 여드름이 있을 때, 알러지가 있을 때 생겨요. Facial flushing occurs when a person is drinking, has a chronic pimples and allergic to something.

⑤ 안면 홍조는 폐경기의 여성에게도 생겨요.

Facial flushing occurs to a woman in menopause.

12) 모공이 뭐예요? What is *Mogong* (pore)?

모공이란 땀구멍이라고도 해요.

The pore is also called 'Sweat hole.'

13) 모공 축소가 뭐예요? What is *Mogon Chukso* (pore minimizing)?

① 모공 축소란 땀구멍의 크기를 줄이는 것이에요.

Pore minimizing is reducing the size of the pore.

② 보통 코 주위의 땀구멍이 큰 경우 모공축소를 해요.

Usually the big pores around the nose get minimized.

14) 잡티가 뭐예요? What is *Japti* (blemish)?

잡티란 얼굴에 생기는 자질구레한 티 또는 흠이에요.

The blemish is small spots in the face.

15) 주름이 뭐예요? What is *Jureum* (wrinkle)?

주름이란 피부에 생긴 줄이에요.

The wrinkle is a line in the skin.

16) 잔주름이 뭐예요? What is a *Janjureum* (fine wrinkle)?

잔주름이란 피부에 생긴 가는 줄이에요.

The fine wrinkle is a thin line in the skin.

17) 주근깨가 뭐예요? What is *Jugeunkae* (freckles)?

주근깨란 얼굴에 생기는 작은 갈색 점이에요.

Freckles are small brown spots in the face.

18) 검버섯이 뭐예요? What is *Geombeoseot* (age spot)?

① 검버섯이란 주로 노인의 살갗에 생겨요.

Age spots usually occurs in the face of old people.

② 검버섯은 피부에 거무스름한 얼룩이 생기는 거예요.

Age spots are blackish stains in the face.

19) 비듬이 뭐예요? What is *Bideum* (dandruff)?

① 비듬은 머리에 생기는 피부병이에요.

Dandruff is a dermatitis in the scalp.

② 비듬은 머리 표면에 회백색 비늘이 생기는 병이에요.

Dandruff is a disease of having light grey scales in the scalp.

20) 튼살이 뭐예요? What is *Teunsal* (chapped skin)?

① 튼살이란 갑작스럽게 살이 쪄서 피부가 터진 모습이에요.

Chapped skin occurs when a person suddenly gained much weight.

② 임신을 하면 배가 트기도 해요.

A pregnant woman usually gets chapped skin.

21) 문신 제거가 뭐예요? What is *Munshin Jegeo* (Removing a tattoo)?

① 문신이란 물감을 이용하여 피부에 그림이나 글씨를 써 넣는 거예요.

Tatoo is a set of pictures or words put on the skin using colors.

② 문신 제거란 문신을 없애는 거예요.

Removing a tattoo is getting rid of the tattoo from the skin.

22) 닭살 피부가 뭐예요? What is *Darksal Pibu* (Goose bumps)?

　　닭살 피부란 털구멍에 각질이 쌓여서 피부가 닭의 살처럼 오돌도돌하게 변한 상태를 말해요.

　　The goose bumps are the state of a skin that becomes grainy just like goose bumps due to the dead skin cells layered in the pores.

23) 백반증이 뭐예요? What is *Baekbanjeung* (leukoplakia)?

　　① 백반증이란 피부에 흰색 반점이 생기는 병이에요.

　　　The leukoplakia is a disease of white spots on the skin.

　　② 백반증은 입술이나 혀에 주로 나타나요.

　　　The leukoplakia occurs on the lips or a tongue.

24) 보톡스가 뭐예요? What is Botox?

　　① 보톡스란 주름을 펴는 주사예요.

　　　Botox is an injection to get a face lift.

　　② 보톡스는 통증감소 효과가 있다고 해요.

　　　Botox has an effect to reduce pain.

25) 노화가 뭐예요? What is *Nohwa* (Aging)?

　　노화란 나이가 들어 여러 기능이 쇠퇴하는 증상이에요.

　　Aging is a symptom of getting old and declined of body functions.

3. 유용한 표현 Useful Expressions

1) 어떤 증상이 있을 때 피부과에 가요?
   When do we go to the dermatology department?

① 여드름이 심하면 피부과에 가요. You should go to the dermatology department when you have serious pimples.

② 화장독이 심하면 피부과에 가요. You should go to the dermatology department when you have serious makeup poison.

③ 기미를 없애고 싶으면 피부과에 가요. You should go to the dermatology department when you want to remove melasma.

④ 털을 없애고 싶으면 피부과에 가요. You should go to the dermatology department when you want to remove unwanted body hair.

⑤ 제모하고 싶으면 피부과에 가요. You should go to the dermatology department when you want to remove hair.

⑥ 아토피가 심하면 피부과에 가요. You should go to the dermatology department when you have serious atopic dermatitis.

⑦ 액취증이 심하면 피부과에 가요. You should go to the dermatology department when you have serious armpit odor.

⑧ 흉터를 없애고 싶으면 피부과에 가요. You should go to the dermatology department when you want to remove scars.

⑨ 안면 홍조가 심하면 피부과에 가요. You should go to the dermatology department when you have serious facial flushing.

⑩ 모공 축소하려면 피부과에 가요. You should go to the dermatology department when you want to diminish the pore.

⑪ 잡티를 없애려면 피부과에 가요. You should go to the dermatology

department when you want to remove blemishes.

⑫ 주름을 없애려면 피부과에 가요. You should go to the dermatology department when you want to remove wrinkles.

⑬ 주근깨를 없애려면 피부과에 가요. You should go to the dermatology department when you want to remove freckles.

⑭ 검버섯을 없애려면 피부과에 가요. You should go to the dermatology department when you want to remove aging spots.

⑮ 비듬을 없애려면 피부과에 가요. You should go to the dermatology department when you want to remove dandruffs.

2) '피부 미용'이 뭐예요? What is *Pibu Miyong* (Skin care cosmetics)?

피부 미용이란 피부를 건강하고 아름답게 하려는 행위를 말해요.

Skin care cosmetics is an activity to keep healthy and beautiful skin.

3) '비만 클리닉'이 뭐예요? What is a *Biman* (obesity) Clinic?

'비만 클리닉'은 살을 빼주는 곳이에요.

An Obesity clinic is a place to help lose weight.

4) '건성'이 뭐예요? What is *Geonseong* (arid)?

① '건성'이란 기름과 땀의 분비가 적은 피부 상태를 말해요.

"Arid" is a state of skin that has little discharge of oil and sweat.

② 건성피부는 건조하고 윤기가 없어요.

The arid skin is dry and has no luster.

③ 건성피부는 얼굴을 씻고 나면 얼굴이 당겨요.

The arid skin gets stiffened after face washing.

5) '지성'이 뭐예요? What is Jiseong (oily)?

① '지성'이란 기름의 분비량이 많은 피부예요.

The oily skin discharges much oil.

② 지성피부는 기름 분비가 많아 여드름이 잘 생겨요.

The oily skin is apt to have pimples.

③ 지성피부는 얼굴을 자주 씻어주면 좋아요.

It is good for the people with oily skin to frequently wash the face.

4. 현장 한국어 Korean in Practice

1) 아픈 증상을 말할 때 이렇게 하세요.

You can talk about your symptoms as follows.

① 여드름이 심해요. I have serious pimples.

② 화장독이 심해요. I have serious makeup poison.

③ 기미를 없애고 싶어요. I want to remove melasma.

④ 털을 없애고 싶어요. I want to remove hair.

⑤ 제모하고 싶어요. I want hair-removing.

⑥ 아토피가 심해요. I have serous atopic dermatitis.

⑦ 액취증이 심해요. I have serious bromhidrosis.

⑧ 흉터를 없애고 싶어요. I want to remove a scar.

⑨ 안면 홍조가 심해요. I have serious facial flushing.

⑩ 모공 축소하고 싶어요. I want to diminish pores.

⑪ 잡티를 없애고 싶어요. I want to remove blemishes.

⑫ 주름을 없애고 싶어요. I want to remove wrinkles.

⑬ 주근깨를 없애고 싶어요. I want to remove freckles.

⑭ 검버섯을 없애고 싶어요. I want to remove age spots.

⑮ 비듬을 없애고 싶어요. I want to remove dandruff.

2) 제 피부 상태가 어때요? How is the state of my skin?

① 건성 피부예요. You have an arid skin.

② 지성 피부예요. You have an oily skin.

③ 건강한 피부예요. You have a healthy skin.

11 치과
Dental Department

1. 핵심어 Key Words

1) 치과 Dental Department

2) 충치 Decayed Tooth

3) 교정 Tooth-Straightening

4) 스케일링 Scaling

5) 임플란트 Implant

6) 사랑니 Wisdom Tooth

7) 치실 Dental Floss

8) 에나멜질 Enamel

9) 상아질 Dentin

10) 발치 Tooth Extraction

11) 불소 도포 Fluorine Application

12) 보존과 Preservation Department

13) 보철과 Dental Prosthetic Department

14) 치주과 Periodontal Department

15) 구강 외과 Dental Surgery

16) 소아 치과 Children's Dentistry

17) 교정과 Correction Department

18) 기공실 Technician's Room

19) 부은 치경 Swollen Teethridge

20) 신경과민 Hypersensitiveness

21) 출혈 Bleeding

22) 틀니(의치) False Teeth (Denture)

23) 치아 검사 Teeth Examination

24) 치조 농누 Pyorrhea Alveolaris

25) 이물감 Foreign Body Sensation

2. 단어 Words

1) 치과가 뭐예요? What is *Chigwa* (Dental department)?

① 치과는 치아와 관련된 병을 치료하는 곳이에요.

The dental department deals with the diseases related with teeth.

② 이가 아프면 치과에 가요.

We should go to the dental department(clinic) when we have a toothache.

2) 치아가 뭐예요? What is *Chia* (tooth)?

① 치아는 '이'라고도 해요.

The tooth is called "*Yee*".

② 치아는 '이빨'이라고도 해요.

The tooth is also called "*Yeepal*".

3) 치과에서는 무엇을 해요? What does the dental department do?

① 충치를 치료해요.

The dental department deals with decayed teeth.

② 치아 교정을 해요.

You can straighten the teeth at the dental department.

③ 스케일링을 해요.

You can have scaling at the dental department.

④ 치아 미백 치료를 해요.

You can have your teeth whitened at the dental department.

⑤ 임플란트를 해요.

You can have implant at the dental department.

⑥ 틀니를 해요.

You can put in the false teeth at the dental department.

4) 충치가 뭐예요? What is *Chungchee* (Decayed tooth)?

① 충치는 벌레 먹은 이에요.

Choongchee is a decayed tooth.

② 벌레 먹은 이는 아프고 이에 구멍이 생겨요.

A decayed tooth has a cavity, and it aches.

5) 치아 교정이 뭐예요? What is *Chia Gyojeong* (Tooth straightening)?

치아 교정이란 비뚤어진 이를 반듯하게 만드는 거예요.

You are wearing braces to straighten the teeth.

6) 스케일링이 뭐예요? What is Scaling?

① 이에 붙어 있는 치석을 없애는 거예요.

Scaling is removing the tartar from your tooth.

② 치석이란 이의 안쪽에 붙어 있는 이물질이에요.

The tartar is a foreign body stuck on the tooth.

7) 치아 미백이 뭐예요? What is *Chia Mibaek* (Tooth whitening)?

치아 미백이란 치아의 표면을 하얗게 만드는 거예요.

You can have your tooth bleached by tooth whitening.

8) 임플란트가 뭐예요? What is Implant?

① 임플란트란 인공 치아예요.

Implant is an artificial tooth.

② 임플란트는 인공치아를 턱뼈에 심는 것이에요.

Implant is planting an artificial tooth in the jawbone.

③ 임플란트는 티타늄으로 만들어요.

Implant is made of titanium.

9) '인공'이 뭐예요? What is *Ingong* (Artificial)?

'인공'은 '사람이 만든 것'이에요.

"Artificial" means "human-made".

10) 틀니가 뭐예요? What is *Teulni* (Artificial tooth)?

① 틀니란 치아가 빠졌을 때 사용하는 인공 치아예요.

You can have a denture (an artificial tooth) when your teeth comes out.

② 틀니는 잇몸에 끼웠다 뺐다 할 수 있어요.

The denture is removable.

11) 치아 이름을 알려 주세요. What are the names of the teeth?

치아 이름 (The names of the teeth)

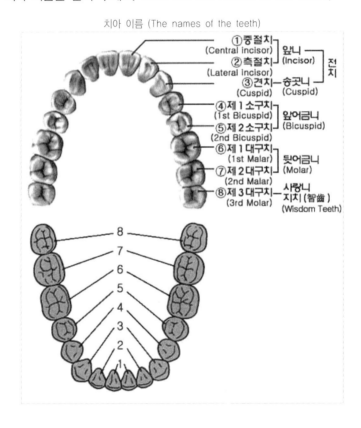

(1) 전치 Front teeth ① 앞니 Incisor ㉮ 중절치 Central incisor

㉯ 측절치 Lateral incisor

② 송곳니=견치 Cuspid

(2) 앞 어금니 Bicuspid ① 제1소구치 First bicuspid

② 제2소구치 Second bicuspid

(3) 뒷 어금니 Molar ① 제1대구치 First molar

② 제2대구치 Second molar

(4) 사랑니 Wisdom teeth ＝제3대구치 Third molar ＝지치 Wisdom teeth

(5) 젖니 Milk tooth

ㄱ 젖니는 아기가 출생한 후 6개월부터~3세 전에 나는 이예요.

Children from 6 months to 3 year old have the milk teeth

ㄴ 젖니는 유아기에 사용한 후 갈게 되요.

The milk teeth change into adult teeth after infancy.

(6) 영구치 : 젖니가 빠진 뒤에 나는 이와 어금니를 말해요.

Children have adult teeth after the milk teeth are removed.

(7) 유치 : 젖니와 같은 말이에요.

Infant teeth are the same with milk teeth.

3. 유용한 표현 Useful Expressions

1) 충치 치료는 어떻게 해요? How can I have a decayed tooth treated?

① 먼저, 이가 아프거나 이에 구멍이 생기면 치괴에 가요.

First, you should go to a dentist when you have a toothache or a cavity in a tooth.

② 의사 선생님께 아픈 곳을 말해요.

You should tell the doctor where it hurts.

③ 그러면 간호사가 먼저 치아 사진을 찍어요.

Then a nurse comes and takes a teeth X-ray.

④ 충치 부위가 적으면 충치를 갈아내고 금이나 아말감으로 때워요.

If the decayed area is small, the dentist removes the decayed area and substitute the area with gold or amalgam.

⑤ 충치 부위가 크면 충치를 갈아내고 금이나 치아색 나는 재료로 씌워요.

If the decayed area is large, the dentist removes the decayed area and coat the tooth with gold or a material with the color of a tooth.

⑥ 충치 먹은 이가 통증이 있으면 신경 치료를 하고나서 씌워요.

If the decayed tooth aches, you will have a root canal and coat the tooth.

⑦ 충치 치료 후에 이가 시리면 다시 치과에 가요.

If you have a toothache after the treatment, you should go to the dentist again.

2) 이는 어떻게 닦아요? How can I brush my tooth?

① 앞니의 뒤쪽을 닦을 때 When brushing the back of the front teeth,
   ㉠ 칫솔을 세로로 잡아요. Take a toothbrush vertically.
   ㉡ 칫솔의 뒷부분을 사용하여 이와 잇몸의 경계선을 닦아줘요.
   Using the toothbrush, you should brush the area between the tooth and the gums.

② 어금니의 혀 쪽을 닦을 때 When brushing the molar inside,
   ㉠ 입을 벌리고 손가락으로 입술을 잡아당겨요.

Open your mouth and pull the lips with your fingers.

ⓛ 칫솔을 비스듬히 넣어 닦아요.

Put in the toothbrush obliquely and brush the inside.

③ 앞니를 닦을 때 When brushing the front teeth,

    ㉠ 칫솔을 나선형으로 움직여 줘요.

    Make spiral movements with the toothbrush.

    ⓛ 한 번에 이 3개를 겨냥해요.

    Brush three teeth at a time.

    ㉢ 한 군데를 10번 정도 솔질해요.

    Brush the same part about ten times.

④ 어금니의 뺨 쪽을 닦을 때 When brushing the molar outside,

    ㉠ 칫솔을 40°로 기울여 넣어요.

    Put in the toothbrush slantly to about 40 degrees.

    ⓛ 이와 잇몸 사이에 솔을 대요.

    Put the brush between the teeth and the gums.

    ㉢ 아래위로 닦아요.

    Brush the tooth up and down.

⑤ 어금니의 맞물림 Occluding of molars

    ㉠ 이가 맞물리는 곳은 상하기 쉬워요.

    The occluding part of the teeth are easy to break.

    ⓛ 앞으로 긁어내는 것처럼 닦아요.

    Brush the teeth just as you are sweeping forward.

3) 어떤 칫솔이 좋아요? What is a good toothbrush?

칫솔은 머리, 칫솔모, 손잡이, 칫솔대 4부분으로 이루어져 있어요.

A toothbrush is composed of head, brush, a grip and a pole.

① 어른 칫솔모 : 가로 15mm, 높이 11mm, 긴 타원형 칫솔모

  The brush for adults : 15mm wide, 11mm high, long oval brush.

② 아기 칫솔모

  ㉠ 솔의 길이는 아기의 위 앞니 2개 길이 정도가 좋아요.

    The brush for a baby should be no wider than the two front teeth.

  ㉡ 솔의 높이는 8mm가 좋아요.

    The heigth of the brush should be 8 mm.

  ㉢ 솔이 길면 잘라 버리세요.

    If the brush is too long, cut it off.

  ㉣ 칫솔 머리가 작고 짧은 것이 좋아요.

    A tooth brush with small and short head is good.

4) 칫솔 관리는 어떻게 해요? How can I manage the toothbrush?

① 이를 닦은 후 칫솔을 흐르는 물에 엄지손가락으로 잘 씻어요.

  After brushing the teeth, wash the brush with running water, using your thumb.

② 칫솔은 통풍이 잘 되는 곳에 세워 둬요.

  Put the toothbrush standing at a place with good ventilation.

③ 칫솔모가 바깥쪽으로 ⅓이상 벌어지면 새 칫솔로 바꿔요.

  If more than a third of brush opens outwardly, you should change it into a new one.

④ 칫솔은 3개월마다 바꾸는 것이 좋아요.

The toothbrush should be changed every three months.

⑤ 칫솔을 소독하고 싶으면 소금물에 담가요.

If you want to sterilize the toothbrush, put it into salt water.

4. 현장 한국어 Korean in Practice

1) 의사 선생님께 어떻게 말해요? How can I say to a dentist?

① 충치가 있어요. I have a decayed tooth.

㉮ 충치 치료해 주세요.

Please take care of my decayed tooth.

㉯ 충치를 아말감으로 때워 주세요.

Please fill the cavity with amalgam.

Please amalgamate the cavity.

㉰ 충치를 금으로 때워 주세요.

Please fill the cavity with gold.

② 이에 음식물이 잘 껴요.

Food particles frequently stuck between the teeth.

③ 앞니가 잇몸 뼈에 박혔어요.

The front teeth are stuck in the gum.

④ 치아 색깔로 씌워 주세요.

Please coat my tooth in the same color.

⑤ 이가 아파요. I have a toothache.

⑥ 이가 흔들려요. My tooth is loose.

⑦ 이가 부러졌어요. My tooth is broken.

⑧ 이가 빠졌어요. My tooth came out.

⑨ 사랑니 빼 주세요. Please take out the wisdom tooth.

⑩ 잇몸이 아파요. My gum hurts.

　㉮ 잇몸이 헐었어요. I have a sore gum.

　㉯ 잇몸이 부었어요. My gum is swollen.

　㉰ 잇몸에서 피가 나요. My gum is bleeding.

　㉱ 잇몸이 파였어요. My gum is torn.

　㉲ 잇몸에 염증이 생겼어요. My gum has inflammation.

　㉳ 의치한 잇몸이 파래요. My gum with denture gets blue.

　㉴ 잇몸을 때워주세요. Please fill in my gum.

　㉵ 잇몸에 고름이 찼어요. My gum is festering.

　㉶ 잇몸 신경치료를 했어요. I had a root canal.

⑪ 치아 교정 해주세요. I want to have my teeth straightened.

⑫ 스케일링 해주세요. My tooth needs scaling.

⑬ 이가 시려요. I feel chills in the teeth.

　㉮ 찬물을 마시면 이가 시려요. I feel chills in the teeth when I drink cold water.

　㉯ 딱딱한 것을 씹으면 이가 시려요. I feel chills in the teeth when I chew a hard thing.

⑭ 미백 치료 해주세요. Please have my teeth whitened.

⑮ 틀니 해주세요. I want to have false teeth.

12

성형외과
Plastic Surgery Department

1. 핵심어 Key Words

1) 성형 Plastic

2) 기형 Deformity

3) 외모 Appearance

4) 이식 Transplant

5) 흡입 Inhalation

6) 개선 Improvement

7) 교정 Correction

8) 장애 Handicapped/ Malfunction

9) 쌍꺼풀 Double Eyelid

10) 이마 Forehead

11) 광대뼈 Cheekbone

12) 매몰법 Investing Method

13) 절개법 Incision

14) 앞트임 Epicanthus Removal

15) 지방 제거술 Liposuction

16) 필러 Filler

17) 콜라겐 Collagen

18) 히알루론산 Hyaluronic acid

19) 안티 에이징 Anti-aging

20) 다크서클 Dark circle

21) 보톡스 Botox

2. 단어 Words

1) '성형외과'가 뭐예요?

What is *Seonghyeon Waegwa*(Plastic Surgery/ Cosmetic Surgery)?

① '성형외과'는 기능 장애를 회복시키기 위해 치료하는 병원이에요.

The plastic surgery deals with the recovery from body malfunction.

② '성형외과'는 외모를 개선하기 위해 치료하는 병원이에요.

The plastic surgery takes care of the improvement of appearance.

③ '성형외과'는 상처를 교정하기 위해 치료하는 병원이에요.

The plastic surgery corrects the scars in the body.

④ '성형'이란 신체 조직을 새로운 모양으로 만드는 것을 말해요.

The plastic surgery is to reshape the body organs.

⑤ '신체 조직'이란 ㉠ 뼈, ㉡ 지방, ㉢ 근육, ㉣ 연골, ㉤ 피부 등을 말해요.

The body organs include ㉠ bone, ㉡ fat, ㉢ muscle, ㉣ cartilage, ㉤ skin

2) 어떤 경우에 성형외과에 가요?

When do we go to the plastic surgery department?

① 비뚤어진 코를 바로 잡으려면 성형외과에 가요.

You should go to the plastic surgery department when you want to straighten the crooked nose.

② 낮은 코를 높이거나 높은 코를 낮추려면 성형외과에 가요.

If you want to raise a low nose or lower a high nose, you should go to the plastic surgery department.

③ 이상한 모양의 귀를 바로 잡으려면 성형외과에 가요.

If you want to correct a strange shape of an ear, you should go to the plastic surgery department.

④ 얼굴이나 목의 주름살을 없애고 싶으면 성형외과에 가요.

If you want to get rid of the wrinkles on the face or the neck, you should go to the plastic surgery department.

⑤ 몸의 지방을 없애고 싶으면 성형외과에 가요.

If you want to remove the fat in the body, you should go to the plastic surgery department.

⑥ 기형의 몸을 바로 잡으려면 성형외과에 가요.

If you want to correct the deformity of the body, you should go to the plastic surgery.

⑦ 화상의 흉터를 없애려면 성형외과에 가요.

If you want to remove a burnscar, you should go to the plastic surgery department.

⑧ 잘려진 손가락, 발가락 등 몸을 붙이려면 성형외과에 가요.

If you want to inosculate the cut off fingers, toes, you should go to the plastic surgery department.

⑨ 유방을 크게 하거나 작게 하려면 성형외과에 가요.

If you want to enlarge or diminish the breast, you should go to the plastic surgery department.

⑩ ㉠ 대머리 때문에 모발 이식을 하려면 성형외과에 가요.

If you want to transplant hair on the bald head, you should go to the plastic surgery department.

㉡ '대머리'란 머리카락에 없는 것을 말해요.

'*Daemeori*(Bald)' means the head has no hair.

㉢ '모발 이식'이란 머리를 두피에 심는 것을 말해요.

'*Mobal Ishik*(The hair transplant)' means planting hair in the scalp.

⑪ 쌍꺼풀 수술을 받으려면 성형외과에 가요.

If you want to have the double eye-lid operation, you should go to the plastic surgery department.

⑫ 보톡스를 맞으려면 성형외과에 가요.

If you want to get a Botox injection, you should go to the plastic surgery department.

㉠ 보톡스를 맞고 싶어요.

I want to get a Botox injection.

㉡ '보톡스'는 주름을 펴는 주사예요.

'Botox' is an injection for a facelift.

⑬ 광대뼈를 없애려면 성형외과에 가요.

If you want to take care of the cheekbone, you should go to the plastic surgery department.

⑭ 턱 모양을 바꾸려면 성형외과에 가요.

If you want to change the shape of the chin, you should go to the plastic surgery department.

⑮ 얼굴에 지방이식으로 살을 붙이려면 성형외과에 가요.

If you want to transplant fat in the face, you should go to the plastic surgery department.

3) '기형'이 뭐예요? What is *Gihyeong* (deformity)?

① '기형'은 신체의 생김새나 기능이 정상과 다른 모습을 말한다.

Deformity is the abnormal state of the body shape or function.

② 기형에는 유전적 기형과 후천적 기형이 있어요.

There are genetic deformity and acquired deformity.

4) '외모'가 뭐예요? What is *Waemo* (appearance)?

'외모'란 겉으로 드러나 보이는 모양을 말해요.

'*Waemo*(Appreance)' is how a person looks.

5) '이식'이 뭐예요? What is *Ishik* (transplant)?

① '이식'이란 '옮겨 심는다'는 뜻이에요.

'*Ishik*(Transplant)' means planting out.

② '장기 이식'이란 살아있는 장기를 떼어내어 나른 사람에게 옮겨 붙이는 일이에요. '*Janggi Ishik*(An organ transplant)' is taking out a living organ from a person and putting it into another person's body.

③ '피부 이식'이란 피부를 떼어내어 다른 곳에 옮겨 붙이는 일이에요

'*Pibu Ishik*(A skin transplant)' is taking out some skin from one part and putting it on another part.

④ '심장 이식'이란 살아있는 심장을 떼어내어 다른 사람의 심장에 옮겨 붙이는 일이에요. '*Shimjang Ishik*(A heart transplant)' is taking out a living heart from one person and putting it into another person's body.

⑤ '신장 이식'이란 어떤 사람의 신장을 떼어내어 다른 사람의 신장에 옮겨 붙이는 일이에요. '*Shinjang Ishik*(A kidney transplant)' is taking out a living kidney of one person and putting it into another person's body.

⑥ '신장 이식'은 '콩팥 이식'이라고도 해요.

A kidney transplant is also called *Kongpat Ishik*.

6) '흡입'이 뭐예요? What is *Heubip* (Inhalation)?

① '흡입'이란 기체나 액체를 빨아들이는 것이에요.

'*Heubip*(Inhalation)' is sucking in gas or liquid.

② '기체'란 수증기처럼 일정한 모양도 없고 부피도 없는 물질이에요.

'*Giche*(Gas)' is a material with no shape and bulk just like vapour.

③ '액체'란 물처럼 일정한 부피는 있지만 모양이 쉽게 바뀔 수 있는 물질이에요. '*Aekche*(Liquid)' is a material with bulk, whose shape is easily changeable.

7) '지방 흡입'이 뭐예요? What is *Jabang Heubip* (Fat inhalation)?

① '지방 흡입'은 몸의 지방을 빼내는 일이에요.

'*Jibang Heubip*(Fat inhalation)' is taking out some fat in the body.

② '지방 흡입술'은 몸의 지방을 빼내는 수술을 말해요.

'*Jibang Heubipsool*(Fat inhalation operation)' is an operation to remove the bodily fat.

8) '지방 제거'가 뭐예요? What is *Jibang Jegeo* (Fat Removal)?

'지방 제거'는 지방을 없애는 것이에요.

'*Jibang Jegeo*(Fat removal)' is removing some fat from a part of body.

9) '개선'이 뭐예요? What is *Gaeseon* (Improvement)?

① '개선'은 잘못된 것을 고쳐 옳은 것으로 만드는 일이에요.

'*Gaeseon*(Improvement) is changing a wrong thing into a correct one.

② '개선'은 나쁜 것을 고쳐 좋은 것으로 만드는 일이에요.

'*Gaeseon*(Improvemtent)' is changing a bad thing into a good one.

③ '개선'은 미운 것을 고쳐 예쁜 것으로 만드는 일이에요.

'*Gaeseon*(Improvemtent)' is changing an ugly thing into a pretty one.

④ '개선'은 불완전한 것을 고쳐 완전한 것으로 만드는 일이에요.

'*Gaeseon*(Improvemtent)' is changing an imperfect thing into a perfect one.

⑤ '개선'은 부족한 것을 고쳐 충분한 것으로 만드는 일이에요.

'*Gaeseon*(Improvemtent)' is changing insufficient thing into a sufficient one.

10) '교정'이 뭐예요? What is *Gyojeong* (Correction)?

① '교정'이란 바르게 고치는 일이에요.

'*Gyojeong*(Correction)' is changing something correct.

② '치아 교정'이란 비뚤어진 이를 똑바르게 만드는 일이에요

'*Chia Gyojeong*(Tooth-straightening)' is arranging the distorted tooth in a straight order.

11) '장애'가 뭐예요? What is *Jangae* (Handicapped)?

① '장애'란 신체적으로 또는 정신적으로 병이 있는 상태를 말해요.
  'Jangae(Handicapped)' is a state of physical or mental disorder.

② '신체 장애'란 몸이 정상 상태가 아닌 경우를 말해요.
  '*Shinche Jangae*(Physically handicapped)' is a state of physical disorder.

③ '정신 장애'란 정신적으로 정상 상태가 아닌 경우를 말해요.
  '*Jeongshin Jangae*(Mentally handicapped)' is a state of mental disorder.

12) '눈썹 문신'이 뭐예요? What is *Nunsseop Munshin* (Eyebrow tattoo)?

'눈썹 문신'이란 눈썹 화장을 한 것처럼 눈썹을 원하는 모양으로 만들어 주는 거예요.
  '*Nunsseop Munshin*(Eyebrow tattoo)' is having a permanent eyebrow makeup using tattoo.

13) '언청이'가 뭐예요? What is *Eoncheongee* (Harelipped)?

'언청이'란 선천적으로 윗입술이 세로로 찢어진 경우를 말해요.
'*Eoncheongee*(Hairlipped)' is a state of a cleft upper lip vertically.

14) '필러(filler)'가 뭐예요? What is filler?

'필러'란 주름이나 흉터 등에 주사하는 물질이에요.
'Filler' is an injection into a wrinkle or a scar.
'필러'에는 콜라겐, 지방, 히알루론산 등이 있어요.
Among the 'filler,' there are collagen, fat, and hyaluronic acid.

15) '필러' 효과는 얼마나 가나요? How long does the 'filler' effect last?

'필러' 효과는 지방이식 효과와 비슷해요.

The 'filler' effect is similar to that of fat transplant.

'필러' 효과는 영구적이 아니에요.

The 'filler' effect isn't permanent.

3. 유용한 표현 Useful Expressions

1) 어느 성형외과가 잘 해요? Where can I find the best plastic surgery?

① 성형외과 잘 하는 곳 아세요?

Do you know where the best plastic surgery is located?

② 좋은 성형외과 소개해 주세요.

Could you introduce to me a good plastic surgery?

2) '정형외과'가 뭐예요?

What is *Jeonghyeong Waegwa* (orthopedics department)?

① '정형외과'는 신체의 기능 장애를 치료하는 병원이에요.

'*Jeonghyeong Waegwa*(An orthopedic department)' deals with the malfunction of the body.

② '정형외과'는 주로 신선성 기형을 치료하는 병원이에요.

'*Jeonghyeong Waegwa*(An orthopedic department)' deals with the innate deformity.

3) '성형외과'와 '정형외과'의 차이가 뭐예요? What is the difference between 'a plastic surgery' and 'an orthopedics department'?

① '성형외과'는 얼굴 부위의 비정상적인 모양새를 고치는 곳이에요. '*Seonghyeong Waegwa*(A plastic surgery)' deals with the abnormal state of the face.

② '정형외과'는 뼈와 근육의 비정상적인 부분을 고치는 곳이에요. '*Jeonghyeong Waegwa*(An orthopedics)' deals with the abnormal states of bones and muscles.

4. 현장 한국어 Korean in Practice

1) 성형외과에 가서 이렇게 말하세요.
Say as follows in a plastic surgery department (hospital).

① ㉠ 코가 비뚤어졌어요. I have a crooked nose.

㉡ 코를 바로 잡아 주세요. Please straighten my nose.

㉢ 코가 낮아요. I have a flat nose.

㉣ 콧대를 세워 주세요. I want to get a nose job to make it sharp.

㉤ 코를 높여 주세요. Please make my nose sharp.

② ㉠ 눈꺼풀이 자꾸 쳐져요. My eyelids often droop.

㉡ 눈꺼풀을 올려 주세요. Please have my eyelids raised.

㉢ 눈꼬리가 쳐져서 졸린 듯해 보여요. Drooped eyelids give me a drowsy look.

㉣ 눈 밑에 지방이 쌓여서 나이 들어 보여요. The face under my eyes makes me look old.

③ ㉠ 귀 모양이 이상해요. My ears look strange.

ⓛ 귀를 예쁘게 고쳐 주세요. Please improve my ear shape.

④ 얼굴 주름을 없애고 싶어요. I want to remove the wrinkles in the face.

⑤ ㉠ 뱃살을 빼고 싶어요. I want to remove the fat in the stomach.

　　ⓛ 지방 흡입 해주세요. I want to have the fat inhaled.

⑥ ㉠ 손가락이 기형이에요. I have a deformed finger.

　　ⓛ 수술해주세요. Please give me a surgery on the deformed finger.

⑦ ㉠ 화상 때문에 흉터가 있어요. I have a burnscar.

　　ⓛ 흉터를 없애주세요. Please remove the scar.

⑧ ㉠ 손가락이 잘렸어요. I had my finger cut.

　　ⓛ 손가락을 붙여 주세요. Please put my finger back.

⑨ ㉠ 유방을 크게 만들어 주세요. I want to enlarge the breast.

　　ⓛ 유방을 작게 만들어 주세요. I want to have a breast reduction operation.

⑩ ㉠ 저는 대머리예요. I'm bald.

　　ⓛ 모발 이식 해주세요. I want to have a hair transplant.

⑪ 쌍꺼풀 수술 해주세요. I want to have double eyelid surgery.

⑫ 보톡스를 맞으러 왔어요. I want to get a Botox injection.

⑬ ㉠ 광대뼈가 많이 나왔어요. I have prominent cheekbones.

　　ⓛ 광대뼈를 낮게 만들어 주세요. Please have my cheekbones flat.

　　ⓒ 광대뼈를 높게 만들어 주세요. Please have my cheekbones prominent

⑭ ㉠ 제 아들이 사각턱이에요. My son has a square jaw.

　　ⓛ 턱을 둥글게 만들어 주세요. Please revise the square jaw round.

⑮ ㉠ 얼굴에 살이 없어요. My face is too skinny.

ⓛ 지방이식으로 살을 붙이고 싶어요. I want to put some flesh on my face through fat transplant.

산부인과
Obstetrics and Gynecology(OB-GYN) Department

1. 핵심어 Key Words

1) 임신 Pregnancy

2) 출산 Parturition

3) 해산 Childbirth

4) 산후 조리 Postpartum Care

5) 수유 Lactation

6) 모유 Breast Milk

7) 우유 Milk

8) 모유 수유 Breast Feeding

9) 기미 Freckles

10) 유산 Miscarrige

11) 조산 Premature Birth

12) 사산 Stillbirth

13) 산전 검진 Before-delivery Exam

14) 빈혈 Anemia

15) 입덧 Morning Sickness

16) 철분제 Iron

17) 초음파 검사 Ultrasonography

18) 태아 Fetus

19) 양수 Amniotic Fluid

20) 촉진제 Parturifacient

21) 진통 Labor Pains

22) 내진 Internal Examination

23) 출산 예정일 Expected Date of Confinement

24) 제왕절개 Cesarean Section

25) 좌욕 Sitz Bath[Hip Bath]

26) 탯줄 Umbilical Cord

27) 회음 절개 Episiontomy

28) 자궁 Womb

29) 폐경 Menopause

30) 피임 Birthcontrol

2. 단어 Words

1) '산부인과'가 뭐예요? What is *Sanbuingwa* (OB–Gyn departmet)?

산부인과는 ㉠ 임신, ㉡ 출산, ㉢ 신생아, ㉣ 부인병 등을 다루는 병원이에요. The '*Sanbuingwa*(OB-GYN)' deals with ㉠ pregnancy, ㉡ childbirth, ㉢ a new-born baby, and ㉣ women's diseases.

2) '임신'이 뭐예요? What is *Imshin* (Pregnancy)?

① '임신'이란 사람이 아이를 가진 것을 말해요.

'*Imshin*(Pregnancy)' is a state of a woman having a baby.

② '임신'이란 짐승이 새끼를 밴 것을 말하기도 해요.

'*Imshin*(Pregnancy)' is also a state of an animal having a baby.

3) '임신'하면 어떤 변화가 있어요? What is changing after pregnancy?

① ㉠ '임신'하면 월경이 정지됩니다.

After pregnancy, menstruation stops.

㉡ '월경'은 '생리'라고도 말해요.

'*Weolgyeong*(Menstruation)' is called '*Saengli*(periods).'

㉢ 임신하면 생리 예정일에 생리가 없어요.

When a woman gets pregnant, she has no periods on a due date.

② ㉠ '임신'하면 체온이 높아져요.

When a woman gets pregnant, her body temperature rises.

㉡ 체온이 높아지는 것을 '고온'이라고 합니다.

Rising of body temperature is called '*Go On*(high temperature).'

㉢ 임신하면 고온이 3주 이상 계속됩니다.

When a woman gets pregnant, the high temperature goes on for over three weeks.

③ ㉠ 임신하면 '질'이 부드러워져요.

When a woman gets pregnant, the vagina gets soft.

㉡ '질'이 부드러워지는 이유는 임신하면 혈액순환이 좋아지기 때문이에요. The vagina gets soft because the pregnance improves the blood circulation.

④ 임신하면 질에서 나오는 분비물이 늘어나요.

When a woman gets pregnant, discharges from the vagina increases.

⑤ 임신하면 유방이 팽팽하게 부풀어요.

When a woman gets pregnant, her breast becomes swollen hard.

⑥ 임신하면 몸과 팔다리가 무거워요.

When a woman gets pregnant, she has difficulty moving her limbs.

⑦ 임신하면 소변이 자주 마려워요.

When a woman gets pregnant, she frequently goes to the bathroom.

⑧ 임신하면 변비가 생겨요.

When a woman gets pregnant, she suffers from constipation.

⑨ 임신하면 머리가 어지러워요.

When a woman gets pregnant, she feels dizzy.

⑩ 임신하면 몸이 추웠다 더웠다 해요.

When a woman gets pregnant, she feels cold and hot.

⑪ 임신하면 가슴이 답답해요.

When a woman gets pregnant, she feels heavy in the chest.

⑫ ㉠ 임신하면 얼굴에 기미가 생겨요.

When a woman gets pregnant, she has freckles in the face.

㉡ '기미'란 얼굴에 생기는 갈색 반점이에요.

'*Gimi*(Freckles) means brown spots occurring in the face.

⑬ 임신하면 멀건 물을 토해요.

When a woman gets pregnant, she throws up whitish water.

⑭ ㉠ 임신하면 구역질을 해요.

When a woman gets pregnant, she vomits.

㉡ 구역질이란 먹은 음식이 위로 올라와 입으로 토하는 것을 말

해요.

'*Guyeokjil*(Vomiting)' means throwing up the food you ate before.

⑮ ㉠ 임신하면 입덧을 해요.

When a woman gets pregnant, she has morning sickness.

㉡ 입덧은 임신 2개월 중순부터(7주째부터 : 관계 후 5주) 나타나요

The morning sickness starts from the middle of the second month of pregnancy (7th week: 5 weeks after intercourse).

㉢ 입덧은 4개월 중순(13주 : 관계 후 11주)정도에 사라져요.

The morning sickness disappears in the middle of the fourth month of pregnancy (13th week: 11 weeks after intercourse).

4) '입덧'이 뭐예요? What is *Ipdeot* (morning sickness)?

① '입덧'은 보통 임신 3개월부터 시작해요.

The '*Ipdeot*(morning sickness)' starts from the 3rd week of pregnancy.

② 입덧의 증상은 어떤 냄새를 맡으면 구역질이 나는 거예요.

The symptom of the morning sickness is to feel nausea at a specific smell.

③ 입덧 할 때는 음식을 먹는 즉시 곧바로 토해요.

When you have the morning sickness, you may vomit as soon as you eat food.

④ 입덧 할 때는 갑자기 어떤 음식이 먹고 싶어지면 참기 어려워요.

When you have the morning sickness, you may be impatient to eat specific food.

⑤ 입덧 할 때는 평소에 좋아하지 않았던 음식이 당기기도 해요.

When you have the morning sickness, you may like to eat some food that you didn't like before.

⑥ 입덧 기간에는 먹고 싶은 것만 조금씩 자주 먹는 게 좋아요.

In the morning sickness period, you may as well eat a little food you want frequently.

⑦ 입덧 증세가 심해서 음식은 물론 물조차 먹기 힘들면 병원에 가야 해요.

If your morning sickness becomes so serious that you can't drink water, you have to go to the hospital.

5) '양수'가 뭐예요? What is *Yangsoo* (Amniotic fluid)?

'양수'는 자궁 내의 태아를 둘러싸고 있는 액체예요.

The '*Yangsoo*(amniotic fluid)' is the liquid in which a fetus is brought up in the womb.

6) '태아'가 뭐예요? What is *Taeah* (Fetus)?

'태아'란 아직 태어나지 않은 뱃속의 아기를 말해요.

A '*Taeah*(fetus)' is an unborn baby in the womb of the mother.

7) '자궁'이 뭐예요? What is *Jagoong* (Womb)?

'자궁'은 뱃속에서 태아가 자라는 기관이에요.

'*Jagoong*(A womb)' is an organ in which a baby is brought up.

8) '질'이 뭐예요? What is *Jil* (Virgina)?

'질'은 여성의 생식기를 말해요.

'*Jil*(A vagina)' is a genital organ of a woman.

9) '출산'이 뭐예요? What is *Choolsan* (a childbirth)?

'출산'이란 뱃속에 있는 아이가 자궁 밖으로 나오는 것을 말해요.

'*Choolsan*(A childbirth)' is the process of a new born baby coming out of the mother's womb.

10) '해산'이 뭐예요? What is *Haesan* (parturition)?

① '해산'은 '출산'과 같은 말이에요.

'*Haesan*(Parturition)' is the same with a childbirth.

② '해산'은 아이를 낳는 것을 말해요.

'*Haesan*(Parturition)' also means delivering a child.

11) '신생아'가 뭐예요? What is *Shinsaengah* (A neonate)?

'신생아'는 갓난아이를 말해요.

'*Shinsaengah*(A neonate)' is a new born baby.

12) '부인병'이 뭐예요? What is '*Buinbyeong* (Gynecopathy)'?

'부인병'은 여성 생식기에 생기는 병을 통틀어 이르는 말이에요.

'*Buinbyeong*(The gynecopathy)' refers to all the diseases in the female genital area.

13) '산후 조리'가 뭐예요? What is *Sanhu Jori* (Postpartum care)?

① '산후'는 '아이를 낳은 후'라는 뜻이에요.

'*Sanhu*(Postpartum)' means 'after childbirth.'

② '산후 조리'는 아이를 낳은 아이 엄마의 몸을 보살피는 것이에요.

'*Sanhu Jori*(Postpartum)' is taking care of a mother's health after her childbirth.

③ '산후 조리'는 '산후 몸조리'라고도 해요.

'*Sanhu Jori*(Postpartum)' is also called *Sanhu Mom Jori* (taking care of mother's body after childbirth).

14) '몸조리'가 뭐예요? What is *Mom Jori* (health care)?

'몸조리'는 허약해진 몸의 기운을 회복하도록 보살피는 것이에요.

'*Mom Jori*(health care)' means taking care of one's health weakened after a diseases or sickness.

15) '신생아실'이 뭐예요? What is *Shinsaengah–shil* (New born baby's room)?

'신생아실'은 갓 태어난 아기를 눕혀 놓는 방이에요.

'*Shinsangah-shil*(A newborn baby's room) is a room in which a new born baby is lying and being taken care of.

16) '분만'이 뭐예요? What is *Bunman* (Parturition)?

① '분만'이란 '출산', '해산'과 같은 말입니다.

'*Bunman*(Parturition)' is the same with '*haesan*(childbirth).'

② '분만'은 아기를 낳는 것입니다.

'*Bunman*(Parturition)' is giving birth to a child.

③ '분만'은 2단계로 나누어집니다.

'*Bunman*(Parturition)' is composed of two stages.

④ '1단계 분만'은 아기의 머리가 나올 수 있을 정도로 산모의 자궁 목이 지름 10cm가량 벌어지는 때입니다.

In the first stage, the diameter of the neck of the mother's womb increases up to about 10 centimeters so that the head of a baby may come out of it.

⑤ '2단계 분만'은 아기가 나오는 때입니다.

In the second stage, the baby comes out of the womb of the mother.

17) '산후조리원'이 뭐예요? What is *Sanhoo Joriwon* (Postpartum Care Center)?

'산후조리원'은 돈을 받고 아기와 아기 엄마를 돌봐주는 곳입니다.

'*Sanhoo Joriwon*(The postpartum care center)' is an institute to take care of the mother and the newborn baby with charge.

18) '산후 도우미'가 뭐예요? What is *Sanhu Dowoomee* (Postpartum Helper)?

'산후 도우미'는 돈을 받고 집으로 방문하여 아기와 아기 엄마를 돌보는 사람입니다.

'*Sanhu Dowoomee*(The postpartum helper)' is a person who takes care of a newborn baby and the mother with charge at their home.

19) '수유'가 뭐예요? What is *Sooyou* (Nursing)?

'수유'는 아기에게 젖을 주는 것입니다.

'*Sooyou*(Nursing)' is breast-feeding a baby.

20) '수유실'이 뭐예요? What is *Sooyou-shil* (Nursing Room)?

'수유실'은 아기에게 젖을 줄 수 있게 만들어 놓은 방입니다.

'*Sooyou-shil*(A nursing room)' is a room in which a mother breast-feeds her baby.

21) '모유'가 뭐예요? What is *Moyou* (breast milk)?

'모유'는 '엄마 젖'입니다.

'*Moyou*(The breast milk)' is mother's milk.

22) '우유'가 뭐예요? What is *Wooyou* (milk)?

'우유'는 '소 젖'입니다.

'*Wooyou*(Milk)' comes from a cow.

23) '대기실'이 뭐예요? What is *Daegishil* (waiting room)?

'대기실'은 아기 낳기 전까지 기다리는 방입니다.

'*Daegishil*(The waiting room) is a room in which pregnant women wait before they give birth to a baby.

24) '분만실'이 뭐예요? What is *Bunman-shil* (delivery room)?

'분만실'은 아기 낳는 방입니다.

'*Bunman-shil*(A delivery room)' is a room in which a baby is born.

25) '제왕절개'가 뭐예요? What is *Jewang Jeolgae* (Cesarean section)?

'제왕절개'는 아기 엄마의 배와 자궁을 절개하여 아기를 꺼내는 수술입니다.

'*Jewang Jeolgae*(The Cesarian section)' is an operation to incise a mother's abdomen and womb and take out a baby.

26) '배내 저고리'가 뭐예요? What is *Baenae Jeogori* (newborn baby's jacket)?

① '배내 저고리'는 갓 태어난 아기에게 입히는 옷입니다.

'*Baenae Jeogori* (Newborn baby's jacket)' is a small jacket for a new born baby.

② '배내 저고리'는 3벌 정도 준비합니다.

People prepare about three pieces.

③ '배내 저고리'는 1달 정도 입힙니다.

A baby wears the clothes for a month.

④ '배내 저고리' 세탁은 매일 합니다.

The clothes should be washed everyday.

⑤ '배내 저고리'는 세탁기에 넣어 돌리거나 '유아 세제'로 빤 후 맑은 물에 넣고 삶는 것이 좋습니다.

The clothes should be washed in a washing machine, or boiled in clean water after being washed with a detergent for a baby.

⑥ '삶는다'라는 말은 물에 옷을 넣고 끓이는 것입니다.

The baby's clothes should be washed in the boiling water.

27) '탯줄'이 뭐예요? What is *Taetjul* (Umbilical cord)?

① '탯줄'은 태아와 태반을 연결하는 줄입니다.

'*Taetjul*(An umbilical cord)' is a cord to connect a fetus and the placenta.

② 탯줄은 길이 60cm, 지름 1.3cm 쯤 됩니다.

An umbilical cord is about 60 centimeters long and 1.3 diacentimeter.

28) '태반'이 뭐예요? What is *Taeban* (Placenta)?

'태반'은 태아와 아기 엄마의 자궁을 연결시키는 기관입니다.

'*Taeban*(A placenta)' is an organ to connect a fetus and the mother's womb.

29) '태교'가 뭐예요? What is *Taegyo* (Fetal education)?

'태교'는 아이를 밴 여성이 태아에게 좋은 영향을 주기 위하여 마음을 바르게 하고 좋은 음악을 들으며 좋은 음식을 먹고 자세를 반듯하게 하며 좋은 말을 하는 것이에요.

'*Taegyo*(Fetal education)' is a series of activities for a pregnant woman to do to have good influence on her baby, including preserving right mind, listening to good music, eating good food, taking correct posture and speaking good words.

30) '좌욕'이 뭐예요? What is *Jwayok* (Sitz bath/Hip bath)?

'좌욕'은 36~45°C의 뜨거운 물에 하반신을 담그는 것이에요.

'*Jwayok*(A sitz bath)' is putting the lower part of one's body in a hot bath with 36~45°C-hot water.

31) '산모'가 뭐예요? What is *Sanmo* (a baby delivering mother)?

'산모'는 아기를 갓 낳은 여성을 말해요.

'*Sanmo*(A baby delivering mother)' is a woman who has just delivered a baby.

32) '첫국밥'이 뭐예요? What is *Cheotgukbap* (the first rice and soup)?

① '첫국밥'은 아이를 낳은 여성이 처음으로 먹는 국과 밥을 말해요.

A woman who has delivered a baby eats '*Cheotgukbap*(the first rice and soup).

② 한국의 첫국밥은 미역국과 흰밥이에요.

In Korea, the woman eats white rice and brown seaweed soup.

33) '미역국'이 뭐예요? What is *Miyokguk* (Brown seaweed soup)?

'미역국'은 물에 미역을 넣어 뜨겁게 끓인 국이에요.

'*Miyokguk*(The brown seaweed soup)' is made of brown seaweed boiled in hot water.

한국에서, 아이를 낳은 여성이 처음으로 먹는 식사는 밥과 미역국이에요.

In Korea, rice and brown seaweed soup is the first food eaten by a woman after she has delivered a baby.

한국에서는 생일날 미역국을 먹어요.

In Korea, people also eat rice and brown seaweed soup on one's birthday.

미역은 갈조 식물 미역과에 속하는 한해살이 바닷말이다.

Brown seaweed is an annual sea plant.

미역은 식품 중 가장 강력한 알칼리성 식품이다.

Brown seaweed is the strongest alkali food.

미역은 산후 자궁 수축에 효과가 좋다.

Brown seaweed helps the contraction of the womb.

미역은 지혈 작용을 한다.

Brown seaweed helps stop bleeding.

미역에는 요오드가 많아 피를 맑게 한다.

The Iodine component in brown seaweed clears the blood.

미역에는 칼슘이 많아 뼈를 강하게 한다.

The Calcium component in brown seaweed consolidates the bones.

미역은 찐득찐득해서 위궤양을 치료한다.

The stickiness of brown seaweed helps treat stomach ulcer.

미역은 담배의 독을 몰아낸다.

Brown seaweed removes the poison of cigarette.

미역을 먹으면 쉽게 배가 불러 다이어트 효과가 있다.

The satiety of brown seaweed has a diet effect, because people feel full easily after eating it.

미역은 혈액 속에 있는 지방을 사라지게 한다.

Brown seaweed removes the fat from blood.

미역 뿌리는 천식을 가라앉힌다.

Brown seaweed root soothes asthma.

미역 뿌리는 기침을 가라앉힌다.

Brown seaweed root soothes cough.

미역에는 섬유질이 많아 변비 예방에 좋다.

The fiber components in brown seaweed prevents constipation.

미역은 성질이 차기 때문에 몸에 열이 많은 사람에게 좋다.

Brown seaweed's cold character helps the people with body fever.

34) '유산'이 뭐예요? What is 'Yousan (miscarriage)'?

① '유산'은 태아가 임신한 지 20주가 못 되어 자궁 밖으로 나오는 것이에요.

'Yousan(A miscarriage)' is taking a fetus less than 20 weeks old out of the womb.

② '유산 되었다', '유산 안 되었다'라고 말해요.

We say "the baby is miscarried" or "the baby is not miscarried".

③ 유산에는 '자연 유산'과 '인공 유산'이 있어요.

There are 'a spontaneous miscarriage,' and 'an artificial abortion.'

④ ㉠ '자연 유산'은 피가 나면서 태아에 이상이 생기는 것이에요.

In case of a spontaneous abortion, the pregnancy is terminated with bleeding.

㉡ '자연 유산'이 되면 '애가 떨어졌다'고 말해요.

In case of a spontaneous abortion, people say the woman has a miscarriage.

⑤ ㉠ '인공 유산'은 '임신 중절 수술'을 하는 것이에요.

An artificial abortion is having an operation for an abortion.

㉡ '인공 유산'은 '애를 뗐다'고 말해요.

In case of an artificial abortion, people say she aborted a baby.

36) '조산'이 뭐예요? What is Josan (Premature birth)?

① '조산'은 예정일보다 아이를 일찍 낳는 것이에요.

'Josan(The premature birth)' is to deliver a baby earlier than expected.

② '조산'이 되면 아이는 인큐베이터에 들어가요.

When a baby is delivered earlier than expected, it will go into an incubator.

③ '인큐베이터'는 '보육기'에요.

An incubator is a breeding machine.

37) '이슬'이 뭐예요? What is *Iseul* (Dew)?

① '이슬'은 아기 낳기 하루나 이틀 전에 피가 나는 것이에요.

The '*Iseul*(dew)' here means the bleeding 1~2 days before a childbirth.

② '이슬'은 콧물과 같은 분비물과 함께 피가 나는 것이에요.

The 'dew' is composed of blood and discharge.

③ '이슬이 비친다'라고 말해요.

We say, "I can see some dew".

38) '사산'이 뭐예요? What is *Sasan* (Stillbirth)?

'사산'은 뱃속에서 이미 죽은 태아를 낳는 것이에요.

'*Sasan*(Stillbirth)' is giving birth to a dead baby.

3. 유용한 표현 Useful Expressions

1) 어떤 증상이 있을 때 산부인과에 가요?

When should I go to the OB–GYN department?

① ㉠ '냉'이 심하면 산부인과에 가요.

You should go to the OB-GYN department when you have a stomach chill.

㉡ '냉'이란 아랫배가 차고 계란 흰자 같은 분비물이 나오는 증상이에요. When a woman has a stomach chill, she feels cold in the lower abdomen area, and has discharge like the white part of an egg.

② ㉠ '대하'가 심하면 산부인과에 가요.

You should go to the OB-GYN department when you have serious leukorrhea.

㉡ '대하'란 투명하고 노르스름한 액체 분비물이 나오는 증상이에요.

The leukorrhea is a symptom of discharging transparent and yellowish sticky fluid.

③ 생리가 불규칙하면 산부인과에 가요.

You should go to the OB-GYN department when you have an irregular periods.

④ ㉠ 생리할 때 '생리통'이 심하면 산부인과에 가요.

You should go to the OB-GYN department when you have a serious menstrual pain.

㉡ '생리통'이란 생리할 때 아픈 증상이에요.

A menstrual pain is a pain during the periods.

⑤ 임신을 원하는데 임신이 안 되면 산부인과에 가요.

You should go to the OB-GYN department when you cannot get pregnant despite your wish.

⑥ 성폭행을 당해 성기가 아프면 산부인과에 가요.

You should go to the OB-GYN department when you have a severe pain in the genital area after a sexual assault.

⑦ 임신 기간에 피가 나오면 산부인과에 가요.

You should go to the OB-GYN department when you have bleeding durinng pregnancy period.

⑧ 임신 중에 분비물이 많으면 산부인과에 가요.

You should go to the OB-GYN department when you have too much discharge during pregnancy period.

⑨ 임신 중에 배가 많이 아프면 산부인과에 가요.

You should go to the OB-GYN department to have a serious stomachache.

⑩ 임신 중에 정기 검진을 받으러 산부인과에 가요.

You should go to the OB-GYN department when you take a physical examination.

⑪ 임신 중에 심한 충격을 받은 일이 있으면 산부인과에 가요.

You should go to the OB-GYN department when you have a severe shock during pregnancy.

⑫ 임신 중에 입덧이 심하면 산부인과에 가요.

You should go to the OB-GYN department when you have extraordinary morning sickness.

⑬ 임신 중절 수술을 하려면 산부인과에 가요.

You should go to the OB-GYN department when you want to have an abortion.

⑭ ㉠ 불임 상담을 하려면 산부인과에 가요.

You should go to the OB-GYN department when you want to have a consultation on sterility.

㉡ '불임'이란 아이가 생기지 않는 경우를 말해요.

'*Bulim*(Sterility)' is the state in which a couple cannot have a baby.

⑮ 여성 생식기가 아프면 산부인과에 가요.

When a woman has a pain in her genital area, she should go to the
OB-GYN department.

2) '산후 조리'는 어떻게 해요? How should the postpartum care be done?

① 산모가 있는 방은 따뜻하게 합니다.

The mother's room should be kept warm.

② 산모는 하루에 6번 정도 조금씩 나누어 식사를 합니다.

The mother should have meals six times a day, little by little.

③ 산모는 따뜻하고 부드러운 음식을 먹습니다.

The mother should have warm and soft food.

④ ㉠ 아기 낳은 날과 출산 후 1일째, 산모는 누워서 손발만 움직입
니다.

On the day and after one day of childbirth, the mother lies in
the bed and moves only hands and feet.

㉡ 음식은 '죽', '미역국'과 같은 반유동식을 먹습니다.

She eats soft meals such as porridge and brown seaweed soup.

⑤ 출산 후 2~3일째, 산모는 누워서 몸을 자유로이 움직입니다.

2-3 days after childbirth, the mother can move freely in the bed.

⑥ ㉠ 출산 후 4~6일째, 산모는 실내를 조금씩 걸어 다닙니다.

4-6 days after childbirth, the mother can walk in the room, little
by little.

㉡ 복대를 할 수 있습니다.

She can put on a binder.

㉢ '복대'란 '배에 감는 띠'를 말합니다.

'*Bokdae*(A binder)' is a bandage rolled around the abdomen.

ⓡ 복대를 하면 늘어진 뱃살을 줄일 수 있습니다.

A binder helps reduce the belly flesh.

⑦ 출산 후 10~14일째, 산모는 집안을 조심스럽게 걸어 다닙니다.

10-14 days after childbirth, the mother can carefully walk around the house.

⑧ 출산 후 14일째부터는 따뜻한 물수건으로 몸을 닦아냅니다.

Two weeks after childbirth the mother washes her body with a warm steamed towel.

⑨ 출산 후 3주 또는 20일 이후부터는 머리를 감을 수 있습니다.

Three weeks or 20 days after childbirth, the mother can wash her hair.

⑩ 출산 후 4주 또는 30일 이후부터는 목욕을 할 수 있습니다.

Four weeks or 30 days after childbirth, the mother can take a bath.

⑪ 출산 후 6주 또는 40일 이후부터는 성생활을 할 수 있습니다.

Six weeks or 40 days after childbirth, the mother can have a sexual relationship.

⑫ 출산 후 45일까지는 충분히 휴식을 합니다.

For 45 days after childbirth, the mother should take a long rest.

⑬ ㉠ 출산 후 몸의 부기를 빼기 위해서는 호박으로 만든 음식을 먹습니다.

The mother should eat food made of a pumpkin to reduce the swelling.

㉡ 음식은 따뜻해야 합니다.

The food should be warm.

㉢ '부기'란 몸이 부풀어 있는 상태를 말해요.

'*Boogi*(Swelling)' means swollen state of a body.

⑭ 한국에서는 산모에게 ㉠ 미역국, ㉡ 호박 달인 물, ㉢ 홍어찜, ㉣ 잉어찜 등을 줍니다.

In Korea the woman who delivered a baby is treated with ㉠ brown seaweed soup, ㉡ pumpkin stew, ㉢ steamed skate, ㉣ steamed carp,

⑮ 변비가 심한 산모는 ㉠ 미역국, ㉡ 호박찜, ㉢ 삶은 고구마, ㉣ 삶은 감자, ㉤ 채소, ㉥ 야채 등을 먹습니다.

The woman with severe constipation will have ㉠ brown seaweed soup, ㉡ steamed pumpkin, ㉢ boiled sweet potato, ㉣ boiled potato, ㉤ vegetables, ㉥ greens, etc.

3) '예비 엄마'가 뭐예요? What is *Yebi Eomma* (a reserved mother)?

① '예비 엄마'란 앞으로 엄마가 될 여성을 말해요.
'*Yebi Eomma*(A reserved mother)' is a woman to be a mother.

② 현재 임신 중에 있는 여성을 '예비 엄마'라고 해요.
A pregnant woman is also called a reserved mother.

4) '초음파 검사'가 뭐예요? What is *Choeumpa Geomsa* (Ultrasonography)?

① '초음파 검사'는 초음파를 어떤 부위에 쏘아서 브라운관으로 비추어 보는 검사예요. '*Choeumpa Geomsa*(Ultrasonography)' is an examination to shoot the ultrasonic beam on a specific organ and check it on a screen.

② '초음파 검사'를 하면 태아의 모습을 브라운관으로 볼 수 있어요.
Ultrasonography helps us take a look at the shape of a fetus on the screen.

③ 태아 상태를 살펴보겠습니다.

Let me take a look at the state of the fetus.

④ 양수는 적당합니다.

The amniotic fluid is all right.

⑤ 심장이 뛰는 거 보이시지요?

You can see the heartbeat, can't you?

⑥ 초음파 사진을 가져가시도록 프린트 하겠습니다.

Let me print out the ultrasonic photo.

5) '배란'이 뭐예요? What is *Baeran* (Ovulation)?

① '배란'이란 성숙한 난세포가 난소에서 배출되는 일이에요.

'*Baeran*(Ovulation)' is a process of mature egg being discharged out of the ovary.

② '배란일'이란 난세포가 난소에서 배출되는 날이에요.

'*Baeranil*(The ovulation day)' is the day when the egg comes out of the ovary.

③ '배란일'은 보통 생리 예정일로부터 14일 전이에요.

The ovulation day is 2 weeks before the menstruation day.

④ '배란기'란 난세포가 난소에서 배출되는 시기예요.

The ovulation day is the period in which the egg cell is discharged.

⑤ '배란기'에 성관계를 하면 임신 가능성이 높아요.

If you have a sexual intercourse during the ovulation, the possibility of being pregnant will get higher.

⑥ 생리 예정일로부터 14일 전후 3일 동안은 임신 가능성이 높아요.

3 days before and after the ovulation, a woman can easily become

pregnant.

6) '유방 마사지'가 뭐예요? What is *Yoobang Massage*(Breast massage)?

① '유방'이란 포유동물의 젖이에요.

'*Yoobang*(Breast)' is a mammal's breast.

② '유방 마사지'는 출산 후 젖이 잘 나오도록 따뜻한 수건이나 따뜻한 손으로 가볍게 문질러 주는 거예요.

The breast massage is to slightly rub the breast with a warm towel or hands so that milk may come out easily.

③ '유방 마사지' 할 때는 두 손을 펴서 유방에 대고 위로 쓸어주듯 만져 줍니다.

During the breast massage, the massager should spread both hands on the breast and rub it upwards.

7) '예쁜이 수술'이 뭐예요? What is *Yepeuni Soosul*(Hymen recovery)?

'예쁜이 수술'이란 출산으로 늘어난 질 입구를 작게 만드는 수술이에요.

'*Yepuni Soosul*(The hymen recovery operation)' is to contract the entrance of the vagina, which has expanded after childbirth.

4. 현장 한국어 Korean in Practice

1) 아픈 증상을 말할 때 이렇게 하세요. Say your symptoms as follows.

① '냉'이 심해요. I have chill stomach.

② '대하'가 심해요. I have serious leukemia.

③ 생리가 불규칙해요. My periods are irregular.

④ 생리할 때 '생리통'이 심해요. I have a serious menstrual pain.

⑤ 임신을 원하는데 임신이 안돼요. I can't get pregnant even though I want it.

⑥ ㉠ 성폭행을 당했어요. I've been raped.

　㉡ 검사해 주세요. I want to be examined.

　㉢ 생식기가 많이 아파요. I have a lot of pain in my genital area.

⑦ 임신 했는데 피가 나와요. I'm pregnant and bleeding too much.

⑧ ㉠ 임신 했는데, 분비물이 많아요. I'm pregnant, and have much discharge.

　㉡ 분비물에서 냄새가 나요. My discharge stinks.

⑨ 임신 했는데, 배가 많이 아파요. I'm pregnant, and have a serious stomachache.

⑩ ㉠ 입덧이 심해요. I have serious morning sickness.

　㉡ 입덧을 안 해요. I have no morning sickness.

⑪ ㉠ 임신 했는데, 교통사고를 당했어요. I'm pregnant, and I had a traffic accident.

　㉡ 이상이 있는지 검사받으러 왔어요. I want to get a medical checkup.

⑫ ㉠ 임신 했는데, 성관계를 했어요. I'm pregnant, and had a sexual intercourse.

　㉡ 괜찮을까요? Will it be OK?

　㉢ 괜찮습니다. That's all right.

　㉣ 성관계를 피해야 합니다. You should avoid a sexual intercourse.

⑬ ㉠ 임신 중절 수술하러 왔어요. I'm here for a surgical abortion.

　　㉡ 낙태하러 왔어요. I came here for abortion.

　　㉢ 애를 떼러 왔어요. I want an abortion.

⑭ 불임 상담하러 왔어요. I want consultation for sterility.

⑮ 시험관 아기 시술에 대해 상담하러 왔어요.

　　I want to be advised about tube baby.

2) 태아의 상태에 관한 표현은 다음과 같이 말해요.
　Say about the state of a fetus as follows.

　① ㉠ 이 약을 먹으면 태아한테 해로워요.

　　　This medication is harmful to a fetus.

　　㉡ 이 약은 태아한테 괜찮아요.

　　　This medication is all right for a fetus.

　② ㉠ 술 한 잔 마셨는데 태아한테 이상 없을까요?

　　　I just had a drink. Will it be harmful to the fetus?

　　㉡ 이상 있습니다. Yes, it is harmful.

　　㉢ 이상 없습니다. No, it is all right.

　③ ㉠ 피임약을 먹었는데, 태아한테 이상 없을까요?

　　　I just took a birthcontrol pill. Will it be harmful to the fetus?

　　㉡ 피임약은 태아한테 해롭습니다.

　　　A birthcontrol pill is harmful to the fetus.

　④ ㉠ 태아가 정상인가요? Is the fetus normal?

　　㉡ 태아는 건강합니다. The fetus is healthy.

　　㉢ 태아가 비정상입니다. The fetus is abnormal.

　⑤ ㉠ 아기가 거꾸로 있어요. 제왕절개 해야 합니다.

The fetus is upside down. You have to have a cesarean section.

ⓛ 제왕절개 하고 싶지 않아요.

I don't want to have a cesarean section.

ⓒ 제왕절개 해주세요.

I want to have a cesarean section.

ⓔ 정상분만 하고 싶어요.

I want to have a eutocia(normal delivery).

ⓜ 유도분만 하고 싶어요.

I want to have an induced delivery.

3) '정기검진' 표현은 다음과 같이 말해요.

The followings are some expressions for medical checkup.

① ㉠ 환자분은 매달 정기검진 받으러 오세요.

The patient should visit the hospital for checkup every month.

ⓛ 언제 오면 되나요? When should I come?

② ㉠ 오늘 병원 가니? Are you going to the hospital today?

ⓛ 네, 오늘 정기검진 받으러 가는 날이에요.

Yes. I'm having a check up today.

③ 의사 선생님, 정기검진 받으러 왔어요.

Doctor, I'm here for a checkup.

④ 지난달에는 정기검진을 못 받았어요.

I couldn't have a checkup last month.

⑤ 정기검진을 꼭 해야 하나요?

Do I have to have a checkup?

4) '초음파 검사' 표현은 다음과 같이 말해요.

The followings are some expressions for "Ultrasonography".

① '초음파 검사' 받으러 왔어요. I'm here for '*Choeumpa Geomsa*(an ultrasonography).

② 딸인지 아들인지 궁금해요. I'm wondering if it is a son or a daughter.

③ '초음파 검사' 하지 마세요. Don't take an ultrasonography.

④ 초음파로 우리 아기 보여주세요. Show me my baby by the ultrasonography.

⑤ 이것은 우리 아기 초음파 사진이에요.

This is the photo of my baby taken by the ultrasonography.

⑥ 어디가 머리예요? Where is the head?

5) '출산' 표현은 다음과 같이 말해요.

The followings are some expressions for 'childbirth'.

① 어제 저녁에 이슬이 비쳤어요. I saw some dew last night.

② 양수가 터졌어요. The amniotic fluid has broken.

③ 양수가 새어 나와요. The amniotic fluid is leaking.

④ 아기 낳을 때, 옆에 있어 줘요.

Please, stay by me during the childbirth.

⑤ 아기 낳을 때, 나가 있어요.

Please, stay outside during the childbirth.

⑥ 아기 낳을 때, 손 잡아 줘요.

Please, hold my hands during the childbirth.

⑦ ㉠ 자궁이 안 벌어져요. The womb does not open,

ⓛ 자궁이 벌어졌어요. The womb is open.

⑧ ㉠ 골반이 작아서 밑으로 아기 낳기 어려워요.

  The pelvis is too small to deliver a baby.

  ㉡ 골반이 커서 아기 낳기 수월해요.

  The pelvis is big enough to deliver a baby.

⑨ ㉠ 아기 머리가 보여요.

  I can see the baby's head.

  ㉡ 아기 다리가 보여요.

  I can see the baby's legs.

⑩ ㉠ 진통이 심해요.

  I have a severe labor pain.

  ㉡ 진통이 1분 간격으로 있어요.

  I have a labor pain every minute.

  ㉢ 진통이 그쳤어요.

  The labor pain has stopped.

⑪ ㉠ 숨을 크게 들이 쉬세요.

  Take a deep breath.

  ㉡ 숨을 크게 내쉬세요.

  Breathe out hard.

⑫ ㉠ 남편분이 산모 배를 쓰다듬어 주세요.

  Husband, please rub the wife's abdomen softly.

  ㉡ 남편분이 아기 탯줄 가르세요.

  Husband, please cut off the umbilical cord.

Medical Korean for English Speakers

III. 알아두면 유용한 표현
Useful Expressions

14

입원할 때
Hospitalization

1. 핵심어 Key Words

1) 입원 Hospitalization

2) 여행사 Tourist Company

3) 병원 Hospital

4) 소개 Recommendation

5) 진료 Medical Treatment

6) 외래 진료 Outpatient Treatment

7) 예약 Appointment

8) 준비 Preparation

9) 소견서 Diagnostic Statement

10) 주치의 General Practitioner(GP)

11) 복용 약 Internal Medicine

12) 수술 Operation

13) 수술 동의서 A Written Consent for an Operation

14) 처방전 Prescription

15) 간병인 Sick Nurse

16) 환자 본인 Patient

17) 보호자 Guardian

18) 입원비용 Hospital Charges

19) 진료비 영수증 Medical Treatment Receipt

20) 발급 Issue

21) 재발급 Re-issue

22) 면회 Interview

23) 면회 시간 Interview Hours

24) 중환자실 Intensive Care Unit(ICU)

25) 절대 안정 Absolute Rest

26) 면회 사절 Interviews Declined

27) 병실 Sick Room

28) 독실 Single Room

29) 1인실 1-Bed Room

30) 2인실 Double Room

31) 4인실 4-Bed Room

32) 6인실 6-Bed Room

2. 단어 Words

1) 소개 받다 Recommend

① 장미영 박사님을 소개 받았어요.

Someone recommended Dr. Jang Mi-young at this hospital to me.

② 김철수 박사님께 진료 받고 싶어요.

I want to see Dr. Kim Cheol-soo.

2) 예약하다 Make an Appointment

① 오전으로 예약해주세요. I want to make an appointment in the morning.

② 오후로 예약해주세요. I want to make an appointment in the afternoon.

③ 월요일 오전으로 예약해주세요. I want to make an appointment on Monday morning.

④ 금요일 오후로 예약해주세요. I want to make an appointment on Friday afternoon.

3) 입원하다 Get hospitalized

① 바로 입원이 가능해요?

Can I get hospitalized right away?

② 입원할 때 필요한 서류는 뭐예요?

What are the required documents for hospitalization?

▶ 요일(Days of a week)
① 일요일 Sunday
② 월요일 Monday
③ 화요일 Tuesday
④ 수요일 Wednesday
⑤ 목요일 Thursday
⑥ 금요일 Friday
⑦ 토요일 Saturday
⑧ 주말 Weekend

3. 유용한 표현 Useful Expressions

1) 여행사를 통해 서울 병원을 소개받았습니다.

The tourist company recommended me Seoul Hospital.

① 지금 진료를 받을 수 있어요?

Can I get a medical treatment right away?

② 친구로부터 장미영 선생님을 소개받았어요.

One of my friends recommended me Dr. Jang Mi-young.

③ 김철수 선생님을 추천해 드립니다.

I'll recommend you Dr. Kim Cheol-soo.

④ 장미영 선생님은 매주 월요일 오전에 외래 진료를 하고 계십니다.

Dr. Jang Mi-young takes care of the outpatients every Monday morning.

⑤ 그럼, 화요일 오전 10시 김철수 선생님으로 예약하겠습니다.

Then, let me make an appointment with Dr. Kim Cheol-soo at 10 o'clock, Tuesday morning.

2) 외래 진료 후 바로 입원이 가능합니까?

Can I get hospitalized right after the outpatient treatment?

① 예, 가능합니다. Yes, you can.

② 아니오, 어렵습니다. No, it's impossible.

3) 입원할 때 무엇을 준비해요?

What should I prepare for hospitalization?

① 세면도구를 준비하세요. Bring your toilet articles, please.

② 주치의 소견서를 갖고 오세요. Bring your GP's diagnostic report, please.

③ CT, MRI 진단서를 갖고 오세요. Bring CT, MRI reports, please.

④ 현재 복용하고 있는 약이 있어요? Are you on medication?

⑤ 현재 복용하고 있는 약을 들고 오세요. Bring your present medication.

⑥ 약 처방전을 들고 오세요. Bring your prescription.

4) 수술할 때 보호자가 필요해요? Do I need a guardian?

① 수술하는 경우에는 보호자가 없으면 안 되나요?

Should I be accompanied by a guardian when I get an operation?

② 한국에서는, 환자가 입원하면 보호자가 병원에서 같이 자기도 해요.

In Korea, when a patient gets hospitalized, the guardian stays nights with him or her.

③ 보호자 대신 간병인이 있어도 돼요.

A sick nurse may substitute the guardian.

④ 수술 시에는 반드시 보호자가 필요합니다.

You must have a guardian when you get an operation.

⑤ 보호자는 의사로부터 수술에 관한 설명을 듣고 '수술 동의서'에 사인해야 합니다. The guardian, after hearing the doctor's explanation about the operation, has to sign on the written consent for an operation.

⑥ 환자 본인의 사인만으로도 수술이 가능합니다.

The patient can get an operation after signing on his own.

5) 입원비가 얼마예요? How much is the hospital charge?

① 입원비용은 어느 정도인가요? How much is the hospital charge?

② 진료비 영수증 발급 해주세요. Can I have a receipt for the medical treatment?

③ 진료비 영수증 발급을 부탁합니다. Please issue the receipt for the

medical treatment.

④ 진료비 영수증 재발급을 부탁합니다. Please have the receipt for the medical treatment re-issued.

6) 면회시간은 언제입니까? When are the interview hours?

① 입원 환자의 면회 시간은 언제입니까?

When are the patient's interview hours?

② 중환자실 환자는 절대 안정이 필요합니다.

The patient in the ICU requires absolute rest.

③ 면회 사절입니다.

Interview is declined.

④ 면회 시간에만 면회하세요.

Please interview the patient during the designated interview hours.

⑤ 면회 시간 이외의 면회를 삼가 주시기 바랍니다.

Please abstain from interviewing the patient after the designated interview hours.

⑥ 면회 시간 이외에는 면회하지 마세요.

Please don't interview the patient after the designated interview hours.

⑦ 환자가 면회를 거절합니다.

The patient refuses the interview.

⑧ 환자가 면회를 원하지 않아요.

The patient doesn't want the interview.

⑨ 입원 병실은 1인실, 2인실, 4인실, 6인실 등이 있습니다.

The sick rooms are 1-bed room, double-bed room, 4-bed room and

6-bed room.

⑩ 1인실은 '독실'이라고도 합니다.

The 1-bed room is also called 'a single room'.

15

병명
Name of Disease

1. 노인 관련 용어 Concerning the Old

1) 노인 The Old

2) 요실금 Uracratia

3) 운동 Exercise

4) 노화 방지 Anti-aging

5) 장수 비결 Secret for a Long Life

6) 우울증 Depression

7) 섹스 Sex

8) 노안 Presbyope (Old eyes)

9) 틀니 Denture

10) 난청 Difficulty of Hearing

11) 심장병 Heart Disease

12) 노후생활 Old Age Life

13) 중풍 Stroke

14) 예방 Precaution

15) 치료 Treatment

16) 응급대처 First-aid

17) 한방치료 Oriental Medicine

18) 증상 Symptom

19) 진단 Diagnosis

20) 치매 Imbecility

21) 관절염 Arthritis

22) 운동요법 Exercise Therapy

23) 류마티스 / 류마티스 관절염 Articular Rheumatism

24) 퇴행관절 / 퇴행성 관절염 Regressive Arthritis

25) 골다공 / 골다공증 Osteoporosis

26) 칼슘 Calcium

27) 디스크 Disk

28) 통풍 Gout

2. 병원 시설 용어 Hospital Facilities

1) 병원 Hospital

2) 의원 Clinic

3) 병동 Sick Ward

4) 대기실 Waiting Room

5) 수술실 Operation Room

6) 마취실 Anesthesia Room

7) 입원실 Sick Room

8) 중환자실 Intensive Care Unit (ICU)

9) 엑스레이실 X-Ray Room

10) 검사실 Examination Room

11) 사무실 Administration Office

12) 원장실 Director's Room

13) 부원장실 Vice-director's Room

14) 수납 창구 Reception Desk

15) 의사실 Doctor's Office

16) 간호사실 Nurse's Station

17) 식당 Dining Room

18) 취사실 Kitchen

19) 신생아실 New-born Baby's Room

20) 분만실 Delivery Room

21) 수유실 Nursing Room

22) 약국 Pharmacy

23) 창고 Warehouse

3. 의료 관련 일반 용어 General Medical Terms

1) 구급차 Ambulance

2) 마취 Anesthesia

3) 박테리아성 Bacterial

4) 바이러스성 Viral

5) 균/세균/병원균 Germ

6) 불치 Incurable Disease

7) 중증 Serious Case

8) 풍토병 Endemic Disease

9) 선천성 Congenital

10) 우발적 Accidental

11) 신진대사 Metabolism

12) 치료 불가 Incurable

13) 만성적 Chronic

14) 동맥질환 Arterial Disease

15) 직업병 Industrial Disease

16) 악성 Malignant

4. 질환별 병명 Disease Names

1) 소화기 질환 Digestive Disease

① 위궤양 Stomach Ulcer

② 위염 Gastritis

③ 위장염 Gastroenteritis

④ 위암 Gastric Cancer

⑤ 위산과다 Chlorhydria

⑥ 궤양성 대장염 Ulcerative Colitis

⑦ 식도암 Esophagus Cancer

⑧ 대장염 Colitis

⑨ 치질 Hemorrhoids

⑩ 간경화 Liver Cirrhosis

⑪ 간암 Liver Cancer

⑫ 십이지장염 Gastroduodenitis

⑬ 식도염 Esophagitis

⑭ 식중독 Food Poison

⑮ 위통 Gastralgia

⑯ 복통 Stomachache

⑰ 위경련 Stomach Cramps

⑱ 위하수 Gastroptosis

⑲ 장염 Enteritis

⑳ 장티푸스 Typhoid Fever

㉑ 열대성 설사 Tropical Diarrhea

㉒ 췌염 / 췌장염 Pancreatitis

㉓ 구토증 Nausea

㉔ 구토 Vomit

㉕ 설사 Diarrhea

㉖ 변비 Constipation

㉗ 혈변 Bloody Stool

㉘ 점액변 Mucous Stool

㉙ 악취변 Stinky Stool

㉚ 묽은 변 Diluted(Waterly) Stool

㉛ 부드러운 변 Soft Stool

㉜ 소화불량 Maldigestion

㉝ 위장병 Gastroenterology

㉞ 위장결석 Gastrostone

㉟ 위장통 Gastroenteric Pain

㊱ 위출혈 Gastrorrhagia

2) 호흡기 질환 Respiratory Disease

① 감기 Cold

② 기침 Cough

③ 코막힘 Congestion

④ 건조한 목 Dry Throat

⑤ 한기 Chills

⑥ 열 Fever

⑦ 발열 Attack of Fever

⑧ 황열병 Yellow Fever

⑨ 자반열 Purpura Fever

⑩ 임파선 Lymph

⑪ 임파선열 Lymph Fever

⑫ 장티푸스성열 Typhoid Fever

⑬ 성홍열 Scarlet Fever

⑭ 발진티푸스 Camp Fever

⑮ 건초열 Hay Fever

⑯ 말라리아 Malaria

⑰ 소모열 Hectic Fever

⑱ 고열 High Fever

⑲ 염증성열 Inflammation Fever

⑳ 편도염 Tonsilar Fever

㉑ 폐암 Lung Cancer

㉒ 폐렴 Pneumonia

㉓ 폐결핵 Pulmonary Tuberculosis

㉔ 천식 Asthma

㉕ 기관지 천식 Bronchi Asthma

㉖ 기관지염 Bronchitis

㉗ 폐색전 Pulmonary Thromboembolism

㉘ 폐기종 Pulmonary Mphysema

㉙ 공핵 Donor Nucleus

㉚ 호흡곤란 Dyspnea

3) 피부 질환 Skin Disease

① 피부염 Dermatitis

② 발진성열 Camp Fever

③ 아토피 피부염 Atopic Dermatitis

④ 두드러기 Hives

⑤ 열상 Laceration

⑥ 화상 Burn

⑦ 무좀 Athlete's Foot

4) 이비인후과 질환 Ear, Nose, Throat Disease

① 중이염 Otitis media

② 후두염 Laryngitis

③ 이하선염 Parotitis ; Mumps

④ 축농증 Empyema

⑤ 후각 상실 Loss of the Olfactory Sense

⑥ 이명 Tinnitus

⑦ 이후

⑧ 비혈 Nose Bleeding

⑨ 난청 Deafness

⑩ 실어증 Aphasia

⑪ 실성증 Mental Disorder

⑫ 호흡 정지 Apnoea

⑬ 구내염 Stomatitis

⑭ 아구창/위구창 Thrush

⑮ 알레르기성 비염 Allergic Rhinitis

⑯ 유행성 이하선염 Epidemic Mumps

5) 구강 질환 Oral Disease

① 치과의학 Dental Medicine

② 충치 Decayed Tooth

③ 치조농루 Pyorrhea Alveolaris

④ 치아 교정 Straightening the Tooth

⑤ 치아 표백 Whitening the Tooth

⑥ 치통 Toothache

⑦ 치주염 Periodontitis

6) 눈 질환 Eye Disease

① 백내장 Cataract

② 녹내장 Glaucoma

③ 눈물 Tear

④ 충혈 Blood-shot

⑤ 두통 Headache

7) 심장 질환 Heart Disease

① 심장마비 Cardioplegia/ Heart Attack

② 협심증 Angina Pectoris

③ 뇌졸중 Stroke

④ 혈전증 Thrombosis

⑤ 심장염 Carditis

⑥ 판막증 Valvular Disease

⑦ 심장수축압 Systtolic Pressure

⑧ 심장확장압 Diatolic Pressure

⑨ 뇌심장염 Endocarditis

8) 순환기 질환 Cardiovascular Disease

① 심부전 Heart Failure

② 심장 판막증 Valvular Heart Disease

③ 허혈성 심질환 Ischemic Heart Disease

④ 선천성 질환 Innate Disease

⑤ 부정맥 Arrhythmia

⑥ 고혈압 Hypertension

⑦ 심근경색 Myocardial Infarction

9) 간 질환 Liver Disease

① 간염 Hepatitis

② 알코올 중독 Alcoholism

③ 만성 알코올 중독 Chronic Alcoholism

④ 간경화 Cirrhosis

⑤ 황달 Jaundice

⑥ 수종/부종 Dropsy/ Edema

10) 신장/비뇨기 질환 Kidney/Urologic Disease

① 신장통 Renal Colic

② 신장염 Nephritis

③ 혈뇨 Bloody Urine

④ 빈뇨 Frequent Urination

⑤ 혈뇨증 Hematuria

⑥ 신우염 Pyelitis

⑦ 방광염 Cystitis

⑧ 전립선염 Prostatitis

⑨ 농뇨증 Pyuria

⑩ 요독증 Uremic Poisoning

⑪ 요관 결석 Stone in the Ureter

⑫ 당뇨병 Diabetes

⑬ 급성신부전 Acute Renal Failure

⑭ 만성신부전 Chronic Renal Failure

⑮ 급성 사구체신염 Acute Nephritis

⑯ 요로 결석 Urinary Stone

⑰ 신종양 Renal Tumor

⑱ 전립선암 Prostate Cancer

11) 혈액 질환 Hematic Disease

① 백혈병 Leukemia

② 혈우병 Hemophilia

③ 악성 림프종 Malignant Lymphoma

④ 골수종 Myeloma

12) 뼈/근육 질환 Bone/Muscular Disease

① 골종양 Bone Tuma

② 골다공증 Osteoporosis

③ 류마티스 관절염 Rheumatoid Arthritis

④ 신경통 Neuralgia

⑤ 근육통 Myalgia

⑥ 통풍 Gout

⑦ 관절염 Arthritis

⑧ 류마티스 Rheumatism

⑨ 골수염 Osteomyelitis

⑩ 골절 Fracture

⑪ 탈구 치료 Dislocation Treatment

13) 뇌/신경 질환 Cerebral(Brain)/Neuro Disease

① 신경학 Neurology

② 뇌혈관장애 Cerebrovascular Accident

③ 뇌졸중 Cerebral Apoplexy

④ 뇌성마비 Cerebral Palsy

⑤ 뇌종양 Cerebral Tumor

⑥ 뇌빈혈 Cerebral Anemia

⑦ 뇌내출혈 Intracerebral Hemorrhage

⑧ 뇌출혈 Cerebral Hemorrhage

⑨ 뇌염 Encephalitis

⑩ 뇌척수막염 Cerebrospinal Meningitis

⑪ 파킨슨병 Parkinson's Disease

⑫ 간질 Epilepsy

14) 여성 질환 Women's Disease

① 산욕열 Puerperal Fever

② 부인과 Gynecology

③ 유산 Miscarriage

④ 유방암 Breast Cancer

⑤ 불임증 Sterility

⑥ 자궁암 Uterine Cancer

⑦ 자궁근종 Uterine Myoma

⑧ 자궁 내막증 Endometriosis

15) 신경 내분비 질환 Neurological/Endocrine Disease

① 애디슨병 Addison's Disease

② 쿠싱 증후군 Cushing's Syndrome

③ 당뇨병 Diabetes

④ 고지혈증 Hyperlipemia

⑤ 갑상선암 Thyroid Cancer

16 예방접종
Vaccination

1. 결핵 예방접종 Tuberculosis Vaccination

1) BCG 예방접종은 결핵 예방을 위한 주사이다.

   BCG vaccination is an injection against tuberculosis.

2) BCG 예방접종은 생후 3주 후에 맞춰야 한다.

   BCG should be taken 3 weeks after birth.

3) BCG 예방접종은 일반병원의 경피용과 보건소의 피내용으로 구분된다.

   BCG vaccination has two types ; the skin type for a general hospital and the hypodemic type for a health clinic.

4) 경피용과 피내용의 효과는 거의 차이가 없다.

   There is little difference in the effectiveness of the two types.

5) 경피용은 피내용에 비해 흉터가 적게 남는다.

   The skin type leaves comparatively smaller scar than the hypodemic type does.

6) 경피용은 낱개 포장이다.

The skin type is individually wrapped.

7) 피내용은 포장단위가 10명씩 사용 가능하게 되어 있다.

The hypodemic type is wrapped for 10 people.

8) 결핵은 결핵균에 의한 감염질환이다.

Tuberculosis is an infection by tuberculosis germs.

9) 결핵은 결핵균이 폐를 침범할 뿐만 아니라 뼈나 관절, 뇌 등 신체의 다른 부위에도 영향을 주는 질환이다.

Tuberculosis germs break into the lungs, and have influence on other organs including bones, joints and brain.

2. B형 간염 예방접종 Hepatitis B Vaccination

1) B형 간염 예방접종은 B형 간염을 예방하기 위해 접종하는 것이다.

Hepatitis B Vaccination helps prevent Hepatitis B.

2) B형 간염 예방접종은 태어나자마자 실시하며 3차까지 접종한다.

Hepatitis B Vaccination should be taken right after birth, followed by two more.

3) 엄마가 B형 간염 보균자일 경우는 아기의 출생 직후 12시간 이내에 예방접종을 한다.

If a mother is a carrier of Hepatitis B, the baby should get vaccination within 12 hours of its birth.

4) 아기의 경우는 첫 예방접종 이후 1개월과 6개월 후에 추가 접종을 해야 한다.

After the first vaccination, a baby should get additional vaccinations after 1 and 6 months.

5) B형 간염은 간염 바이러스에 의해 간에 염증이 생기는 병이다.

Hepatitis B is a viral inflammation that takes place in the liver.

6) B형 간염에 걸리면 지속적인 황달이 나타나며 피로하고 식욕이
부진해지는 증상이 나타난다.

Hepatitis B is followed by the jaundice, fatigue and loss of appetite.

7) 한국인은 인구의 5~8% 정도가 B형 간염에 감염되어 있는 것으
로 조사되고 있다.

It is reported that about 5-8 percent of Korean population is
infected with hepatitis B.

8) B형 간염은 한번 걸리면 완치가 어려우므로 예방접종만이 최선
의 예방책이다.

As hepatitis B is not perfectly cured once infected, vaccination is the
best precaution.

9) B형 간염은 수혈이나 오염된 주사기에 찔리는 경우에 감염되기
쉽다.

Hepatitis B is transmitted by blood transfusion and contaminated
needles.

10) B형 간염은 투석, 오염된 한방 침, 시술 등에 의해 감염되므로
반드시 일회용 주사기나 일회용 침을 사용해야 한다.

As hepatitis B is transmitted by hemodialysis, contaminated acupuncture
needles and treatment, disposal needles should be used.

11) B형 간염은 성관계, 육체적 접촉 등에 의해서도 감염될 수 있다.

Hepatitis B can be transmitted by sexual intercourse or other
physical contacts.

12) B형 간염에는 신생아가 엄마로부터 감염되는 신생아 수직 감염도 있다.

Among hepatitis B, there is a vertical transmission, which means a direct infection from a mother to a newborn baby.

3. 디프테리아, 파상풍, 백일해 예방접종
Vaccinations for Diphtheriae, Tentanus, Pertussis

1) 디프테리아, 파상풍, 백일해 예방접종은 DTap 예방접종을 통해 예방할 수 있다.

Vaccinations for diphtheriae, Tantanus and Partussis are taken through DTap vaccination.

2) DTap 예방접종은

As for DTap vaccination,

① 모든 신생아에게 생후 2, 4, 6개월에 3회 기초 접종을 해야 한다.

a basic vaccination should be given 3 times within 2, 4, 6 months after birth.

② 생후 15~18개월, 만 4~6세에 각각 1회 추가 접종을 해야 한다.

additional vaccination should be given within 15-18 months and the ages of 4-6 after birth.

③ 만 11~12세에 Tdap 또는 Td 백신으로 1회 접종을 해야 한다.

At the age of 11-12, the children should be vaccinated with Tdap or Td vaccination.

④ 총 3회의 기초 접종과 만 4~6세 추가 접종은 DTap-IPV 혼

합백신으로 접종이 가능하다

3 initiative basic vaccinations and additional vaccinations at the age of 4-6 can be prescribed with the combination of DTap-IPV.

3) DTap 백신도 심한 알레르기 반응과 같은 이상 반응을 일으킬 수 있지만 매우 드물다.

DTap vaccination may cause some allergic reactions, which are rare.

4) DTap 백신은 건강한 상태에서 접종받는 것이 중요하다.

It is important to take a DTap vaccination in a healthy condition.

5) DTap 백신 접종은 접종 전에 반드시 의사의 예진을 받아야 한다.

Before taking DTap vaccination, a patient should be diagnosed by a doctor.

6) DTap 백신 접종 후에는 30분간 접종기관에 머물러 몸 상태를 관찰해야 한다.

After taking DTap vaccination, the patient should stay in the clinic for 30 minutes to observe the body condition.

7) DTap 백신 접종 후에는 집에 돌아간 후에도 3시간 정도 주의 깊게 몸 상태를 관찰해야 한다.

After taking DTap vaccination, the patient should observe the body condition with care for about 3 hours after arriving at home.

8) DTap 백신 접종 후에는 3일간 특별한 관심을 가지고 몸 상태를 관찰해야 한다.

After taking Dtap vaccination, the patient should observe the body condition with special care for 3 days at home.

9) DTap 백신 접종 후에 고열이 있거나 평소와 다른 신체증상이 나타나면 곧바로 의사의 진료를 받아야 한다.

If high fever or any other unusual symptoms are found, the patient should go to a doctor right away.

10) DTap 백신 접종 후의 흔한 이상 반응은 접종 부위의 통증, 부어오름, 발열, 보채기, 식욕부진, 구토 등이다. 흔한 이상 반응은 일반적으로 7일 이내에 자연적으로 증상이 좋아진다.

Some common unusual reactions after DTap vaccination include pain, swelling and fever in the injected area, impatient crying, loss of appetite, and vomiting. Such reactions are to get better naturally within 7 days.

11) DTap 백신 접종 후의 드문 이상 반응은 40.5도 이상의 심한 고열, 3시간 이상 심하게 보채기, 발작성 경련, 심한 두드러기 등이다.

Some unusual reactions after DTap vaccination include high fever with over 40.5 degrees body temperature, impatient crying over 3 hours, a fit of convulsion and serious rashes.

드문 이상 반응이 나타나면 관할 보건소에 신고하거나 예방접종 도우미 사이트의 '이상 반응 신고하기'를 통해 신고한다.

When such unusual reactions are found, we should report them to a local clinic or through the vaccination web-site.

드문 이상 반응에 대해서는 의사의 진료를 받아야 한다. 이때 의사에게 이상반응 증상과 증상이 발현된 시간, 예방접종 시간 등을 알려 주어야 한다.

The unusual reactions should be taken care of by a doctor. The patient should inform the doctor of the symptom, time of appearance, and vaccination time.

12) DTap 백신 접종 후의 아주 드문 이상 반응은 호흡이 가쁘고 쉰 목소리가 나며 쇼크에 빠지는 것이다.

Some very rare unusual reactions after DTap vaccination include panting, getting hoarse voice and being shocked.

13) 디프테리아는 디프테리아 균이 인두와 편도에 염증을 일으켜 호흡장애를 일으키는 병이다.

Diphtheria is a respiratory disturbance resulted from the inflammation in the pharynx and the throat caused by diphtheria germs.

14) 디프테리아는 호흡기로 배출되는 균이나 피부병변 등의 접촉으로 전파된다.

Diphtheria is transmitted by the germs discharged through respiratory organ or contacts on the sore skin.

15) 파상풍은 파상풍 균이 신경 독성 물질을 분비하여 근육을 마비시키고 입을 열거나 삼키기 어렵게 하며, 호흡 마비, 전신 마비 등을 일으키는 병이다.

Tetanus germs produce poisonous material to neuro-system, paralyze muscles and make it difficult for a patient to open the mouth or swallow, causing respiratory and body paralysis.

16) 파상풍은 파상풍 균이 토양에 존재하며 오염된 상처를 통해 전파된다.

The tetanus germs exist in the soil, and transmitted through contaminated scars.

17) 백일해는 백일해 균이 호흡기 염증을 일으켜 심한 기침 발작을 유발하는데, 이러한 증상이 수 주간 지속될 수 있는 병이다.

Pertussis patient has inflammation in the respiratory organ, which causes serious cough, and such symptoms may last for several weeks.

18) 백일해는 기침이나 재채기 등 호흡기 전파가 주된 경로이다.

Pertussis is mainly transmitted through respiratory activities such as cough and sneezing.

4. 소아마비(폴리오) 예방접종
Vaccination for Infantile Paralysis (Polio)

1) 소아마비(폴리오) 예방접종은 모든 영유아를 대상으로 생후 2, 4, 6개월에 3회 기초 접종을 한다.

All the babies should have basic vaccination against polio 3 times, in the 2nd, 4th and 6th months after birth .

2) 3차 접종 가능 시기는 생후 6~18개월까지이다.

The third vaccination can be taken in 6-18 months after birth.

3) 소아마비(폴리오) 예방접종은 만 4~6세 때 1회 추가 접종한다.

Children at the ages of 4-6 will have additional vaccination.

4) 소아마비(폴리오) 예방접종은 접종 후 경미한 통증과 부종이 있을 수 있다.

After the vaccination, children may have slight pain and swelling.

5) 소아마비(폴리오)는 사람에서 사람으로 직접 감염되는데, 특히 분비물이나 입을 통해 감염된다.

Polio is transmitted personally, through discharge or a mouth.

6) 소아마비(폴리오)는 95% 이상이 별다른 증상 없이 감염되었다가 감기처럼 가볍게 앓고 나서 회복된다. 1% 미만의 감염자에게 이완성 마비가 나타난다.

95 % of polio cases are recovered without any specific symptom after inflammation, just like a slight cold. Less than 1 percent of infected people may have a paralysis.

5. 홍역 예방접종 Measles Vaccination

1) 홍역 예방접종은 생후 12~15개월에 첫 접종을 한다.

   Measles vaccination is taken first between 12th and 15th months after birth.

2) 홍역 예방접종은 만 4~6세 때 두 번째 백신을 접종한다.

   The second measles vaccination is given to a patient at the ages of 4-6.

3) 홍역 예방접종은 1차 접종 후 잊고 있다가 초등학교 입학 때 접종 확인서를 제출함으로 인해 2차 접종을 받는다.

   When a child goes to an elementary school, he or she has to hand in the record of the 1st vaccination. After that the child will get the 2nd vaccination.

4) 홍역이 유행하는 경우는 12개월 미만의 영아들의 경우 1차 접종 이전, 2차 접종을 기다리는 만 4~6세 아이들이 위험에 노출되기 쉽다.

   When measles prevails, children under 12 months are to be exposed to the disease before their first vaccination, and those at the ages of 4 to 6 may be exposed to the disease while they are waiting for the second vaccination.

5) 홍역 예방접종은 1차의 경우 90%, 2차의 경우 99%의 예방 효과

가 있다.

As for the measles vaccination, the first one has 90 percent and the second one has 99 percent of prevention effect.

6) 만일 홍역 환자와 접촉한 경우에는 6일 이내에 면역 글로블린을 접종 받는다.

Whoever contacted a measles patient should be vaccinated with immune Globlin within 6 days.

7) 해외여행을 할 때, 생후 12~15개월 이전의 영아는 출국 전 1차 접종을 받아야 하며, 4~6세 아이들의 경우에는 2차 접종을 미리 맞아야 한다.

For an oversea travel, children between 12 months and 15 months old have to get the first vaccination before they leave the country, and the children between 4 and 6 years old should get the second vaccination beforehand.

8) 홍역은 한번 걸린 후 회복되고 나면 평생 다시 걸리지 않는다. 하지만 예방접종을 받은 후 10년이 지나면 3% 정도의 사람들이 홍역에 걸릴 수 있다. 따라서 어른들의 경우에는 적절한 간격으로 예방접종을 다시 받는 것이 좋다.

The measles never repeats in one's lifetime after it has been cured. However, after ten years of vaccination, about 3 percent of people can get down with the disease. Therefore, adults are requested to get vaccinations in proper intervals.

9) 예방접종 여부가 불확실한 경우에는 해외여행 이전에 백신 2회 접종을 완료하거나 적어도 1회 이상 백신을 접종하고 출국해야 한다.

If state of vaccination is not clear, it is advised that one take 2 vaccinations, or at least one, before leaving the country.

10) 해외여행 이후 1~2주 이내에 발열, 발진이 발생하면 꼭 병원을 방문하여 정확한 진단을 받아야 한다.

If one has fever or rashes within 1-2 weeks after overseas travel, one should go to a doctor for an exact diagnosis.

11) 홍역이 발병하면 38도 이상의 고열과 함께 기침, 콧물, 설사 증상이 나타난다.

The symptoms of the measles include cough, nasal congestion and diarrhea along with high fever over 38℃.

12) 홍역이 발병하면 볼에서부터 발진이 나타나며 증상이 심해지면 발진이 볼에서 목, 팔, 몸통, 발 순으로 퍼지게 된다.

When the measles starts, rashes are found from one's cheeks, and if the symptom gets worse, they spread from the cheeks to the neck, arms, body and feet.

13) 어른들의 경우 홍역이 발병하면 아이들보다 더 증상이 심하다.

When an adult has the measles, his symptoms are much worse than those of children.

14) 홍역은 바이러스 감염으로 발생한다. 주로 기침이나 재채기를 통하여 전파된다.

The measles comes from the viral infection, which is transmitted through coughs and sneezes.

15) 홍역은 매우 강한 급성 발진성 바이러스 질환이므로 홍역 환자를 접촉한 경우 90% 이상 홍역이 발병한다. 특히 홍역에 감염된 사람이 자리를 떠난 이후에도 바이러스가 2시간 이상 공기

에 존재한다.

The measles is a very acute viral infection and if one contacts a patient he or she will have the disease in over 90 percent of the cases. Even after the patient leaves the place, the virus exists for over 2 hours.

6. 유행성 이하선염(볼거리) 예방접종 Mumps Vaccination

1) 유행성 이하선염(볼거리) 예방접종은 생후 12~15개월에 1회 접종한 후 만 4~6세 때 또 1회를 접종한다.

Children are first vaccinated against mumps 12-15 months after birth, and second at the age of 4-6.

2) 유행성 이하선염(볼거리) 예방접종 후에는 통증, 두통, 발열, 발진이 나타날 수 있다.

After vaccination, body aches, headache, fever and rashes may happen.

3) 유행성 이하선염(볼거리)에 감염되면 귀밑, 턱밑, 혀밑에 있는 침샘이 부어오르면서 아프다.

Mumps may cause swelling and pain in the salivary glands under the ear, the jaw and the tongue.

4) 유행성 이하선염(볼거리)은 타애과의 접촉을 통해서 일어난다.

Mumps is caused by a contact with saliva.

5) 유행성 이하선염(볼거리) 발병 초기에는 1~2일간 발열, 두통, 근육통, 식욕부진, 구토 증상이 나타난다. 그런 후에 한 쪽 또는 양쪽 볼이 1주일 정도 붓는 증상이 지속된다.

At the early stage, mumps causes 1-2 days of fever, headache, muscular pain, anorexia and nausea. Then both cheeks are swollen for about a week.

6) 유행성 이하선염(볼거리)은 특별한 치료 방법이 없다. 대다수의 환자가 자연 치유된다. 통증이 심한 경우는 진통제를 투여한다.
Mumps has no special treatment. Most cases are cured naturally. When the patient has a severe pain, he can take a painkiller.

7. 풍진 예방접종 Rubella(German Measles) Vaccination

1) 풍진 예방접종은 결혼하기 전 최소 3개월 전에 하는 것이 좋다.
Rubella vaccination should be taken at least 3 months before marriage.

2) 풍진 예방접종을 하고 나서는 최소 3개월 동안 피임해야 한다.
After rubella vaccination, pregnancy should be avoided for at least 3 months.

3) 풍진에 걸리면 임파선이 붓고 열이 나고 관절염 증세가 나타난다.
Rubella causes swelling and fever in the lymph glands.

4) 풍진은 바이러스성 감염으로 기침이나 재채기에 의해 감염되는 전염병이다.
Rubella is a viral infection transmitted by coughing or sneezing.

5) 산모가 풍진에 걸리면 기형아가 발생된다.
If a mother is infected with rubella, the baby may become malformed.

6) 풍진은 감염된 뒤 증상이 일어나기까지 잠복기 기간이 2~3주이다. 하지만 증상이 드러나는 기간은 3~4일로 짧다. 그래서 풍진은 3일 정도만 지나면 없어진다 하여 '3일 홍역'이라고도 한다.
It takes 2-3 weeks for the symptoms of rubella to take place, but

they last only 3-4 days. As rubella disappears in three days, it is also called a 'three day measles.'

8. 수두 예방접종 Chicken Pox Vaccination

1) 수두 예방접종은 생후 12~15개월에 1회 접종한다.

A Chicken pox vaccination is taken once within 12-15 months after birth.

2) 수두 예방접종 후에는 접종 부위가 붓거나 아프거나 발열, 발진이 발생할 수 있다.

After the vaccination, swelling, pain, fever and rashes may take place.

3) 수두는 발진이 생기기 1~2일 전부터 전염력이 있으니 이 기간 동안에는 외출을 하지 않아야 한다.

Chicken pox can be transmitted even 1-2 days before the rashes appear, so the patient should stay inside.

4) 수두로 인한 모든 상처는 깨끗이 관리하고 2차 감염이 되지 않도록 주의한다.

All the injuries caused by chicken pox should be managed clearly, and the patients should be careful not to get a second infection.

5) 수두는 기침이나 재채기 또는 물집의 직접 접촉에 의해 감염된다.

Chicken pox can be transmitted by coughing, sneezing and a direct contact with the blisters.

6) 수두에 걸리면 급성의 미열이 나고 발열, 피로감을 호소하며 피부 발진이 시작된다. 물집은 3~4일 동안 지속되며 7~8일 내에 딱지를 남기고 호전된다. Chicken pox is followed by an acute

fever, fatigue and skin rashes. The blisters last for 3-4 days, and will get better in 7-8 days, leaving dried scabs.

9. 일본 뇌염 예방접종 Japanese Encephalitis Vaccination

1) 일본 뇌염 예방접종은 사백신 접종과 생백신 접종으로 나눈다. WHO와 질병관리본부에서는 사백신을 권장한다.

There are two kinds of Japanese Encephalitis vaccination; dead vaccination and live vaccination. World Health Organization(WHO) and Korea Centers for Disease Control and Prevention(KCDCP) recommend the dead vaccination.

① 사백신 접종은 생후 12~24개월에 1주일 간격으로 2회 접종한다. 3차 접종은 2차 접종 후 12개월 뒤에 한다. 만 6세, 만 12세 때 각각 1회 접종한다. The dead vaccination is taken twice at an interval of a week within 12-24 months after birth. The third vaccination should be taken 12 months after the second vaccination. It should be vaccinated once again respectively at the ages of 6 and 12.

② 생백신 접종은 생후 12~24개월에 1회 접종하고 12개월 후에 2차 접종하며 만 6세 때 3차 접종한다. The live vaccination can be taken once within 12-24 months after birth, the second vaccination should be taken 12 months after the first one, and the third one should be taken at the age of 6.

2) 일본 뇌염 예방접종 후에는 통증, 주사 부위 부어오름, 발열, 발진이 발생할 수 있다. The Japanese Encephalitis vaccination may

cause a pain, swelling, fever and rashes.

3) 일본 뇌염은 작은 빨간 집모기인 일본 뇌염 모기가 산란기에 감
염된 돼지를 흡혈한 후 사람을 무는 과정에서 전염된다.

The Japanese Encephalitis is transmitted by a Japanese Encephalitis
mosquito, which is a red house mosquito, when it bites a person
after sucking the blood of a pig.

4) 일본 뇌염은 모기 활동이 많은 여름철과 초가을에 많이 발생한다.

The Japanese Encephalitis happens in summer and early fall, when
the mosquitoes are activated.

5) 일본 뇌염은 전 연령층에서 발생하나 15세 이하에서 70~80% 발
생하고 고령층에서 주로 발생한다.

The Japanese Encephalitis can occur in all age groups, 70~80
percent of which occurs to the people under the age of 15, and
mostly old ages.

6) 일본 뇌염은 감염 모기에 물린 후 7~20일 후에 증상이 시작된다.

The symptoms of Japanese Encephalitis starts about 7-20 days after
the mosquito bite.

7) 일본 뇌염은 처음에는 95% 무증상이다. 그러나 일단 뇌염이 발
병하게 되면 사망률이 5~30%이다. 회복이 되더라도 후유증이
있다.

95 percent of the Japanese Encephalitis has no symptoms at first.
However, once it occurs, its death rate is 5-30 percent. Even though
it is recovered, it has side effects.

8) 일본 뇌염은 4~14일의 잠복기를 지나 급성으로 발병된다. 발병
초기에는 고열, 두통, 현기증, 구토 혹은 흥분상태 등이 나타난

다. 병이 진행되면 의식장애, 경련, 혼수상태가 일어난다. 회복기에는 언어장애, 판단능력 저하, 사지운동 저하 등 후유증이 나타난다.

The Japanese Encephalitis develops acute after 4-14 days of latency. In the beginning, it is accompanied by high fever, headache, dizziness, nausea and extreme nervousness. As the disease develops, it is accompanied by unconsciousness, convulsion and coma. In the periods of recovery, such symptoms as a speech impediment, lacking in judging ability, and inactiveness of the limbs appear.

9) 일본 뇌염의 가장 확실한 예방은 모기에 물리지 않도록 하는 것이다.

The surest way to prevent the Japanese Encephalitis is not to be bitten by a mosquito.

10. 인플루엔자(독감) 예방접종 Influenza(Flu) Vaccination

1) 인플루엔자(독감) 예방접종은 1년 1회 정도 인플루엔자 바이러스 백신 주사가 권장되고 있다.

The influenza (Flu) vaccination is taken in an injection type once a year.

2) 인플루엔자(독감)는 A, B, C형으로 분류되는 바이러스에 의해 생긴다. 인플루엔자 A형은 2, 3년을 주기로 나타나고, 인플루엔자 B형은 4, 5년을 주기로 나타난다.

The influenza (Flu) occurs from the virus in the types of A, B and C. The influenza A comes at intervals of 2 or 3 years, and influenza B comes at intervals of 4 or 5 years.

3) 인플루엔자(독감)는 모든 연령층에서 나타나지만 소아기나 청년기에 가장 많이 나타난다.

The influenza (Flu) occurs in every age group, mostly in infancy and adolescence.

4) 인플루엔자(독감)는 대개 추운 계절에 더 많이 발생한다.

The influenza (Flu) occurs mostly in a cold weather.

5) 인플루엔자(독감)는 기침이나 재채기를 할 때 나오는 감염된 작은 물방울을 들이마심으로써 사람에서 사람으로 호흡기를 통해 전염된다.

The influenza (Flu) is transmitted from a person to another through the respiratory organs when one inhales very small infected water drops coming out of a patient's coughing or sneezing.

6) 인플루엔자(독감)에 걸리면 오한, 피로, 근육통 등의 증세가 갑자기 시작된다.

The influenza (Flu) causes acute chills, fatigue and muscular pain.

7) 인플루엔자(독감)에 걸리면 체온이 38~40도로 급격히 상승한다.

The influenza (Flu) also causes the acute high fever by 38~40 degrees celsius.

8) 인플루엔자(독감)에 걸리면 머리가 아프고 온몸에 심한 근육통이 생기며 목 부위가 따끔거리는 증상이 나타난다.

The influenza (Flu) causes headache, sever muscular body ache, and sore throat.

9) 인플루엔자(독감)에 걸리면 쇠약감과 무력증이 오래 지속된다.

The influenza (Flu) causes a long period of weakness and helplessness.

10) 인플루엔자(독감)에 걸리면 누워서 쉬거나 아스피린을 사용하여

해열시켜야 한다.

When one is taken up with the influenza (Flu), one should lie down to take a rest or take some aspirin to lower the fever.

11. 감기 예방접종 Cold Vaccination

1) 감기와 독감은 직접 관련이 없다.

A cold is not directly related with the flu.

2) 독감 예방접종으로는 감기를 예방할 수 없다.

The flu vaccination cannot prevent a cold.

3) 감기는 콧물, 재채기, 코막힘으로 시작하여 기침으로 진행된다. 큰 합병증 없이 1주일 정도 지나면 자연 치유된다.

A cold starts with runny nose, sneezing and nasal congestion followed by cough. It will be cured in a week without a big complication.

3) 감기는 감기 바이러스가 돌연변이를 하기 때문에 예방접종약을 만들기 어렵다. 따라서 치료약도 없다. 항생제도 감기의 치료약이 될 수 없다.

As a cold virus mutates, it is difficult to make a vaccine against it. There is no perfect medicine for a cold, and even the antibiotics cannot be a perfect medicine.

4) 감기는 면역력이 저하된 사람들에게 걸리기 쉽다. 감기를 예방하기 위해서는 비타민 먹기, 나쁜 공기 피하기, 과로하지 않기, 잘 자기를 실천해서 예방 면역력을 만들어야 한다.

People with low immunity are apt to catch a cold. Therefore, in order to prevent a cold, one should raise the immunity by taking vitamins and sound sleep, and by avoiding bad atmosphere and overworking.

12. 장티푸스 예방접종 Typhoid Vaccination

1) 장티푸스 예방접종은 만 5세 이상 접종이 가능하며 기초 접종 1회 실시 후 3년마다 추가 접종을 해야 한다.

   The typhoid vaccination can be given to the children over 5 years old. After one basic vaccination, the child has to take additional vaccination every three years.

2) 장티푸스 예방접종은 특히 식품위생업소나 급수시설 종사자, 급식소 조리사 등에게 필요하다.

   The typhoid vaccination is necessary for the people working in food and hygiene facilities, water supply facilities, and the cooks in feeding facilities.

3) 장티푸스 예방을 위해서는 평소에 손씻기를 생활화하여 개인위생을 철저히 해야 한다.

   In order to prevent the typhoid, we should make sure personal hygiene, washing hands frequently.

4) 장티푸스 예방을 위해서는 물은 끓여서 마시고 음식물은 60도 이상에서 10분 이상 가열한 익힌 음식을 섭취하는 것이 좋다. 장티푸스를 유발하는 살모넬라균은 70도 이상에서 1~2분 정도 가열해야 방지할 수 있다.

   Water should be boiled before drinking, and all the food should be heated over 60 degrees celsius for over 10 minutes. The salmonella virus can be killed when it is exposed to the heat over 70 degrees celsius for 1~2 minutes.

5) 해외여행을 계획 중인 경우에는 장티푸스 예방을 위해 여행 2주 전에 장티푸스 예방접종을 하는 것이 좋다.

If you are planning an overseas trip, you'd better get a typhoid vaccination about 2 weeks before the trip.

6) 장티푸스는 물을 통하여 전염되는 질환이다.

The typhoid is transmitted through water.

7) 장티푸스는 비위생적인 물이 섞인 바다에서 자란 굴 등과 같은 어패류, 갑각류, 오염물이 묻은 과일, 장티푸스 환자가 조리한 음식, 장티푸스 보균자의 배설물에 오염된 음식을 섭취했을 때 감염된다.

The typhoid occurs when one eats the fish and shells grown in unhygienic water, contaminated fruit, the food cooked by the typhoid patient or the food contaminated by the typhoid carrier's excrement.

8) 장티푸스는 보통 1~3주의 잠복기를 거쳐 발열, 복통, 무기력증, 식욕부진, 느린 맥박, 설사 또는 변비 증상이 나타난다. 발병 후 2~3주 뒤부터는 탈진과 40도를 오르내리는 고열 등의 증상이 나타나며 몸에 장미 모양의 발진이 피면서 피가 섞인 변이 나온다.

The typhoid occurs after 1-3 weeks of latency along with fever, stomachache, helplessness, loss of appetite, slow pulse, diarrhea or constipation. In 2-3 weeks, dehydration and high fever over 40 degrees celsius appear accompanied by rose-shaped rashes on the body and bloody stools.

17 의사와 환자의 대화
Conversations between a Doctor and a Patient

1. 의사 선생님 말씀 Doctor's Comments

1) ① 어디가 아프세요? Where does it hurt?

　　② 가슴이 아파요. I have a pain in the chest.

2) ① 아픈 데를 손으로 짚어 보세요. Please point where it hurts with your hand.

　　② 여기가 아파요. It hurts right here.

3) ① 언제부터 아팠어요? When did it begin to hurt?

　　② 2월부터 아팠어요. Since February.

4) ① 얼마만큼 아파요? How much does it hurt?

　　② 망치로 때리는 것처럼 아파요. I have a hammering pain.

5) ① 얼마나 자주 아파요? How often does it hurt?

　　② 식사 때마다 아파요. It hurts every mealtime.

6) ① 언제 가장 많이 아파요? When does it hurt most?

　　② 밤에 더 아파요. It hurts most at night.

▸ How many months are there in a year? (1년에 몇 개월이 있습니까?)

1월 : January
2월 : February
3월 : March
4월 : April
5월 : May
6월 : June
7월 : July
8월 : August
9월 : September
10월 : October
11월 : November
12월 : December

7) ① 식욕은 좋으세요? Do you have good appetite?

② 식욕이 없어요. I've lost appetite.

8) ① 또 다른 데, 아픈 곳 있어요? Does it hurt anywhere else?

② 등도 아파요. My back hurts, too.

9) ① 오늘은 어떠세요? How is it, today?

② 오늘은 덜 아파요. It's less painful.

10) ① 오늘 기분 어때요? How do you feel, today?

② 우울해요. I feel blue

11) ① 오늘 대변 보셨나요? Did you have bowels movements, today?

② 아직 못 봤어요. No, I didn't yet.

12) ① 소변은 잘 나와요? Do you urinate well?

② 소변이 잘 안 나와요. I can't urinate well.

13) ① 전에도 아픈 적이 있어요? Have you ever been sick?

② 전에는 건강했어요. I was healthy in the past.

14) ① 수혈 받은 적 있어요? Have you ever received a blood transfusion?

② 수혈 받은 적 없어요. I haven't received a blood transfusion.

15) ① 입원하셔야 해요. You'd better get hospitalized.

② 알겠어요. I see.

16) ① 상태를 봐야 하니까 이삼일 입원 하세요. Please stay in hospital for 2-3 days so that we can check your state.

② 알겠어요. I see.

17) ① 지금 검사 해봅시다. Let's examine it.

② 알겠어요. I see.

18) ① 지금 즉시 수술을 해야 합니다. You have to get an operation right now.

② 알겠어요. O.K., I see.

19) ① 마취를 해야 합니다. You have to get anesthesia.

② 전신 마취를 합니다. You have to get general anesthesia.

③ 부분 마취를 합니다. You have to get local anesthesia.

④ 마취 주사를 놓습니다. I'll give you an anesthetic injection.

20) ① 임신 중이에요? Are you pregnant?

② 네, 임신 중이에요. Yes, I am.

③ 아니오. No, I'm not.

21) ① 알레르기 있어요? Are you allergic to anything?

② 네, 주사 알레르기 있어요. Yes, I'm allergic to injection.

③ 알레르기 있는지 없는지 몰라요. I have no idea.

22) ① 엑스레이 찍으세요. Take an X-ray, please

② 단추를 풀고 가슴을 열어 주세요. Unbutton the shirt and open your chest.

③ 브래지어를 벗으시고 가슴을 열어 주세요. Take off the brasier and open the chest.

④ 상의를 벗고 가운을 입으세요. Take off the jacket and put on a gown.

⑤ 하의를 벗고 가운을 입으세요. Take off the pants and put on a gown.

⑥ 위를 보고 누우세요. Lie down on your back.

⑦ 돌아 누우세요. Turn around.

⑧ 방향을 바꾸세요. Change directions.

⑨ 오른쪽을 보고 누우세요. Lie down to look at the right.

⑩ 왼쪽을 보고 누우세요. Lie down to look at the left.

⑪ 숨을 깊게 들이쉬세요. Take a deep breath.

⑫ 숨을 멈추세요. Hold your breath.

⑬ 숨을 크게 내쉬세요. Breathe out a big breath.

⑭ 옷 입으세요. Put on the clothes.

23) ① 열을 잴게요. Let me take a temperature.

② 맥을 볼게요. Let me check your pulse.

③ 혈압을 잴게요. Let me check your blood pressure.

④ 소변을 받아 오세요. Take your urine.

　　이 컵에 소변을 받아 오세요. Take your urine in this cup.

⑤ 대변을 받아 오세요. Take your stool.

⑥ 가래를 받아 오세요. Take your phlegm.

⑦ 혈액 검사 합니다. Let's have a blood test.

⑧ 피부 검사 합니다. Let's have a skin test.

⑨ 조직 검사 합니다. Let's have a tissue test.

⑩ 혈액형 검사 합니다. Let's check the blood type.

⑪ 심전도 검사 합니다. Let's have an ECG(Electric cardiogram)

test.

⑫ 초음파 검사 합니다. Let's take an ultrasonography.

⑬ 채혈 합니다. Let me take a blood sample.

⑭ 팔을 걷어 주세요. Roll up the sleeve.

⑮ 힘을 빼세요. Relax.

24) ① 주사 놓습니다. I'll give you an injection.

② 소매를 걷어 주세요. Roll up the sleeve.

③ 솜으로 누르고 계세요. Press hard with a cotton ball.

④ 문지르지 마세요. Don't rub it.

⑤ 마사지 해주세요. Just have a massage.

⑥ 긁지 마세요. Don't scratch.

⑦ 오늘은 목욕하지 마세요. Do not take a bath today.

⑧ 오늘은 술 마시지 마세요. Do not drink today.

⑨ 홍역 예방주사 맞았나요? Have you taken the measles vaccination?

⑩ 간염 예방주사 맞았나요? Have you taken the hepatitis vaccination?

⑪ 감기 예방주사 맞았나요? Have you taken the flu vaccination?

2. 환자 말씀 Patient's Comments

1) ① 병명이 뭐예요? What's the name of the disease?

② 어디가 아파요? Where does it hurt?

2) ① 왜 아파요? Why does it hurt?

② 아픈 원인이 뭐예요? What's the cause of the pain?

3) ① 언제쯤 나을까요? When can I recover?

② 언제쯤 좋아질까요? When can I get better?

③ 낫는데 얼마나 걸려요? How long will it take for me to recover?

④ 좋아지는데 얼마나 걸려요? How long will it take for me to get better?

4) ① 직장에 나가도 괜찮을까요? Is it all right if I go to work?

② 언제부터 일을 시작할 수 있어요? When can I resume my work?

③ 완쾌될 수 있나요? Can I recover completely?

④ 재발하지 않나요? Will it not recur?

(나아도 재발하는 경우가 있습니다. It may recur after the

recovery.)

⑤ 부작용은 없어요? Aren't there any harmful side effects?

⑥ 수술 후유증은 남지 않나요? Aren't there any harmful side effects after the operation?

5) ① 수술 안하면 안 될까요? Can I avoid the operation?

② 약으로 치료할 수 있을까요? Will it be cured with medicine?

③ 자연요법으로 치료할 수 있나요? Will it be cured with naturopathy?

6) ① 어떤 것을 먹어야 할까요? What should I eat?

② 물 마셔도 될까요? Can I drink water?

③ 약은 언제 먹어요? When should I take the pills?

④ 약은 몇 번 먹어요? How often should I take the pills?

⑤ 약은 언제까지 먹어요? Until when should I take the pills?

7) ① 이 주사는 왜 맞아요? What is this injection for?

② 꼭 주사를 맞아야 하나요? Do I have to take this injection?

③ 주사 안 맞으면 안 될까요? May I avoid the injection?

④ 주사 알레르기가 있어요. I'm allergic to injections.

8) ① 꼭 입원해야 하나요? Do I have to be hospitalized?

② 언제까지 입원해야 하나요? Until when should I stay in hospital?

③ 퇴원해도 될까요? May I leave the hospital?

④ 퇴원하고 싶어요. I want to leave the hospital.

9) ① 화장실에 데려다 주세요. Please take me to the bathroom.

② 병실이 추워요. The patient's room is too cold.

③ 병실이 더워요. The patient's room is too hot.

④ 병실이 건조해요. The patient's room is too dry.

⑤ 병실이 습해요. The patient's room is humid.

⑥ 창문 좀 열어 주세요. Please open the window.

⑦ 물 좀 주세요. Please give me some water.

⑧ 침대 좀 올려 주세요. Please raise my bed.

⑨ 침대 좀 내려 주세요. Please lower my bed.

⑩ 산책하고 싶어요. I want go out for a walk.

⑪ 밖에 나가고 싶어요. I want to go out.

⑫ 휠체어 좀 갖다 주세요. Please bring me a wheelchair.

10) ① 수술은 얼마나 걸려요? How long will the operation take?

② 수술비용이 얼마예요? How much is the operation fee?

③ 언제쯤 회복되나요? When can I get recovered?

④ 언제쯤 퇴원하나요? When can I leave the hospital?

⑤ 부작용은 없어요? Aren't there any harmful side effects?

⑥ 완치가 가능해요? Can I get completely cured?

⑦ 재발하지 않나요? Does it not recur?

11) ① 파스 붙여도 되나요? Can I put pain relief patch?

② 목욕해도 되나요? Can I take a bath?

③ 밥 먹어도 되나요? Can I eat rice?

④ 술 마셔도 되나요? Can I drink alcohol?

⑤ 물 마셔도 되나요? Can I drink water?

⑥ 수면제 먹어도 되나요? Can I take sleeping pills?

⑦ 비타민 먹어도 되나요? Can I take vitamins?

⑧ 샤워해도 되나요? Can I take a shower?

⑨ 머리 감아도 되나요? Can I wash my hair?

⑩ 걸어 다녀도 되나요? Can I walk around?

⑪ 닭고기 먹어도 되나요? Can I eat chicken?

⑫ 진정제 먹어도 되나요? Can I take a sedative?

⑬ 찜질해도 되나요? Can I take a steam bath?

⑭ 한약 먹어도 되나요? Can I take oriental medicine?

12) ① 겨우 걸어 다닐 수 있을 정도예요. I can just manage to walk.

② 일어서기가 힘들어요. I am hardly able to stand on my feet.

③ 걷기가 힘들어요. I can hardly walk.

④ 걸을 수 없어요. I can't walk.

⑤ 일어설 수는 있어요. I can just stand on my feet.

⑥ 일어설 수는 있지만 걸을 수는 없어요. I can stand on my feet, but I can't walk.

18 약
Medication

1. 약에 관한 용어 Terminology for Medication

1) 약국 Pharmacy

① 약국으로 가세요. Please go to the pharmacy.

② 약 타가지고 가세요. Please get your medicine at the pharmacy.

2) 투약 Medication

① 투약하겠습니다. Let me put in the medicine.

② 1시간 후에 투약하겠습니다. Let me put in the medicine in an hour.

3) 주사약 Injection

① 주사약을 3cc[삼 시시] 놓겠습니다. Let me put in 3cc of injection.

② 새로 나온 주사약입니다. This is a new type of injection.

4) 바르다 Apply

① 약을 바르세요. Apply the medicine.

② 약을 골고루 펴서 잘 바르세요. Apply the medicine evenly and carefully.

③ 약을 너무 많이 바르지 마세요. Don't apply too much medicine.

④ 약을 바르고 문지르세요. Don't rub after application.

5) 붙이다 Patch

① 약을 붙이세요. Please patch the medicine.

② 약을 붙이고 누워 계세요. Lie down and relax after patching the medicine.

6) 식전 복용 Take before Meals

① 식전에 복용하세요. Take it before meals.

② 약은 식사하기 전에 드세요. Take your medicine before meals.

③ 식후에 복용하세요. Take it after meals.

④ 약은 식사한 후에 드세요. Take the medicine after meals.

⑤ 약은 식사하시고 30분 후에 드세요. Take the medicine 30 minutes after meals.

⑥ 약은 식간에 드세요. Take it between meals.

⑦ 약은 자기 전에 드세요. Take the medicine before you go to bed.

⑧ 약은 3시간마다 드세요. Take the medicine every three hours.

⑨ 약은 필요할 때마다 한 알씩 드세요. Take one pill as necessary.

⑩ 약은 하루에 한 번 드세요. Take it once a day.

⑪ 약은 매 끼마다 두 알씩 드세요. Take two pills after each meal.

⑫ 약은 아침에 한 번, 저녁 식사 후에 한 번 드세요. Take the medicine once in the morning and once after dinner.

⑬ 약은 6개월간 꾸준히 드셔야 합니다. You have to take the medicine reqularly for six months.

⑭ 약은 5시간 간격을 두고 드셔야 합니다. You have to take the medicine every five hours.

⑮ 약은 의사의 지시에 따라 드셔야 합니다. You have to take the medicine as directed by the doctor.

2. 약의 형태에 따른 용어 Types of Medicine

1) 가루약 Powdered Medicine

2) 환약 A Globule

3) 알약 A Pill

4) 정제 A Tablet

5) 물약 Liquid Medicine

6) 시럽 Syrups

7) 캡슐 Capsule

8) 연고 Ointment

9) 파스 Patch

10) 반창고 Adhesive Plaster

11) 좌약 Suppository

12) 도포제 Embrocation

13) 내복약 Internal Medicine

14) 외용약 External Remedies

3. 내복약 Internal Medicine

1) 진통제 Pain Reliever

2) 진정제 Sedative

3) 기침약 Cough Medicine

4) 감기약 A Cold Medicine

5) 심장약 A Heart Medicine

6) 해열제 Antifebrile

7) 강압제 Hypotensor

8) 지혈제 Hemostatic

9) 이뇨제 Diuretics

10) 항이뇨제 Antidiuretic

11) 소화제 Digestive Medicine

12) 수면제 Sleeping Pills

13) 영양제 Nutritional Supplement

14) 비타민 Vitamins

15) 항생제 Antibiotic

4. 외용약 External Remedies

1) 소독제 Antiseptic

2) 안약 Eye Drops

3) 양치약 Collutory

4) 세안약(洗眼藥) Eye Wash

4. 약 관련 단어 Medicine Related Words

1) 원내 처방 Intrahospital Prescription

2) 원외 처방 Extrahospital Prescription

3) 대체 조제 Alternative Prescription

4) 조제실 Dispensary

5) 조제약 Pharmaceutic

6) 약국 Pharmacy

7) 약사 Pharmacist

8) 처방전 Prescription

19 체질
Constitution

1. 핵심어 Key Words

1) 체질 Constitution/Physioligical Types

2) 음식 Food

3) 추위 Cold

4) 더위 Hot

5) 태양인 *Taeyang* Type

6) 태음인 *Taeeum* Type

7) 소음인 *Soeum* Type

8) 소양인 *Soyang* Type

9) 소식 Eating Small Meals

10) 과식 Overeating

11) 폭식 Excessive Eating

12) 사상 체질 Four Physiological Types

13) 침 Acupuncture

14) 뜸 Moxa

15) 한약 Oriental Medication

16) 한의학 Oriental Medicine

17) 기공 Qigong

18) 소극적 Passive

19) 적극적 Active

20) 보수적 Conservative

21) 진보적 Liberal

22) 내성적 Reserved/Introvert

23) 외향적 Extrovert

24) 독재적 Authoritative

25) 민주적 Democratic

26) 건조하다 Dry

27) 습하다 Moist/Humid

28) 손이 차다 Cold Hands

29) 발이 뜨겁다 Hot Feet

30) 땀이 많다 Excessive Sweating

31) 땀이 적다 Little Sweating

32) 땀이 없다 No Sweating

33) 상체 Upper Body

34) 하체 Lower Body

2. 단어 Words

1) 체질에 맞는 음식을 알려 주세요.
Tell me about the foods suitable to my physiological type.

① 체질에 맞는 음식을 드세요.

You should eat the foods suitable to your physiological type.

② 체질에 맞은 음식은 체질에 따라 다른가요?

Are there any specific foods suitable to specific physiological type?

2) 추위에 약한 편이세요? Are you oversensitive to cold weather?

① 추위에 약한 편이에요. I am oversensitive to cold weather.

② 더위에 약한 편이에요. I am oversensitive to hot weather.

③ 추위를 잘 견뎌요. I can stand cold weather.

④ 더위를 잘 견뎌요. I can stand hot weather.

⑤ 추위를 잘 타요. I am sensitive to cold weather.

⑥ 더위를 잘 타요. I am sensitive to hot weather.

3) 체질에 따라 달라요. It depends on the physiological type.

① 체질에는 태양인, 태음인, 소음인, 소양인의 4가지가 있어요.

There are four physiological types : *Taeyang, Taeeum, Soeum, Soyang.*

② 손발이 찬 편이에요. I have cold limbs.

③ 식사를 급하게 해요. I eat fast.

④ 소식해요. I eat little.

⑤ 과식하는 편이에요. I have a habit of overeating.

⑥ 자주 폭식해요. I'm a glutton.

⑦ 거식증이 있어요. I am anorexic.

4) 손발이 따뜻해요. I have warm limbs.

① 손발이 따뜻한 편이에요. My limbs are warm.

② 손발이 찬 편이에요. My limbs are cold.

③ 손가락이 갸름해요. My fingers are thin.

④ 겨울에는 손발이 쉽게 건조해져요. My limbs get dry in winter.

⑤ 손발이 따뜻하나 힘이 없어요. My limbs are warm but weak.

⑥ 비교적 땀이 많은 편이에요. I sweat a lot.

⑦ 조금만 걸어도 땀이 많이 나는 편이에요. I sweat a lot after a short walk.

⑧ 상체가 길고 하체가 짧아요. I have a long upper body and short lower body.

⑨ 상체가 짧고 하체가 길어요. I have a short upper body and long lower body.

⑩ 손 힘이 약해요. I have a weak grip.

⑪ 손이 차서 악수하기가 미안해요.

I feel sorry in handshaking because my hands are so cold.

5) 외모가 어때요? How is the appearance?

① 뼈가 가늘어요. My bones are thin.

② 날씬해요. I am slim.

③ 어깨가 넓어요. I have broad shoulders.

④ 어깨가 떡 벌어졌어요. The shoulders are broad./I am well-built.

⑤ 체격이 커요. He has a big constitution.

⑥ ㉠ 이목구비가 커요./작아요. She has big/ small features.

㉡ 눈이 커요./작아요. The eyes are big/ small.

㉢ 코가 커요./작아요. The nose is big/ small.

㉣ 콧구멍이 커요./작아요. The nostrils are big/ small.

㉤ 입술이 두꺼워요./얇아요. The lips are thick/ thin.

㉥ 입이 커요./작아요. The mouth is big/ small.

㉦ 귀가 커요./작아요. The ears are big/ small.

㉧ 손이 커요./작아요. The hands are big/ small.

㉨ 발이 커요./작아요. The feet are big/ small.

㉩ 엉덩이가 커요./작아요. The hip is big/ small.

㉪ 키가 커요./작아요. I am tall/ short.

㉫ 뚱뚱해요./홀쭉해요. I am fat/ slender.

㉬ 살 쪘어요./말랐어요. I am plump/ skinny.

㉭ 머리가 커요./작아요. The head is big/ small.

⑦ ㉠ 얼굴이 갸름해요. The face is slender.

㉡ 얼굴이 계란형이에요. The face is oval.

㉢ 얼굴이 둥근 형이에요. The face is round.

㉣ 얼굴이 넓적해요. The face is flat.

㉤ 얼굴이 네모 형이에요. The face is angled.

㉥ 얼굴이 삼각형이에요. The face is triangular.

㉦ 얼굴이 역삼각형이에요. The face is reversed triangular.

㉧ 얼굴이 마름모 형이에요. The face is diapered.

㉨ 얼굴이 길어요./짧아요. The face is long/ short.

㉩ 얼굴색이 어두워요./밝아요. The face is dark/ bright.

㉪ 얼굴이 통통해요./수척해요. The face is chubby/ gaunt.

ⓟ 얼굴에 살이 없어요./살이 많아요. The face is thin/ plump.

ⓗ 얼굴에 혈색이 없어요./혈색이 좋아요.

　　The complexion is pale/ sanguine.

⑧ 턱이 뾰족한 편이에요./둥근 편이에요.

　　He is lantern-jawed/ round-jawed.

⑨ 이마가 넓어요./좁아요. He has a broad/ narrow forehead.

⑩ 광대뼈가 나왔어요./광대뼈가 들어갔어요.

　　He has prominent/ flat cheekbones.

⑪ 눈빛이 강해요./약해요. He has a strong/ weak expression.

⑫ 피부가 두꺼워요./얇아요. The skin is thick/ thin.

⑬ 피부가 약해요./강해요. The skin is weak/ strong.

⑭ 얼굴색이 흰 편이에요./가무잡잡한 편이에요./검은 편이에요./붉은 편이에요./노란 편이에요./푸른 편이에요.

　　The complexion is whitish/ darkish/ reddish/ yellowish/ bluish.

⑮ 몸에 지방이 많아요./적어요.

　　He has a lot of/ little fat in the body.

6) 행동이 어때요? How does he behave?

① 남과 시선 마주치기를 싫어해요.

　　He doesn't like to see others face to face.

② 걸음이 느려요./빨라요. He walks slowly/ fast.

③ 무게 있게 걸어요./가볍게 걸어요.

　　He walks with dignity/ flippantly.

④ 몸을 좌우로 흔들며 걸어요./반듯하게 걸어요./팔자 걸음이에요./십일자 걸음이에요./오리걸음이에요.

He walks swaying side to side./ He walks straightly./ He has a swaggering gait./ He has a straight walking./ He walks like a duck.

⑤ 걸음걸이가 꼿꼿해요./허리를 구부정하게 구부리고 걸어요.

He walks with his back straight./ He walks with a slight stoop.

7) 성격이 어때요? How is his character?

(1) 성격이 좋아요./성격이 나빠요. He has a good/ bad character.

① 보수적이에요./진보적이에요. He is conservative/ liberal.

② 변화를 싫어해요./변화를 좋아해요.

He doesn't like/ likes changes.

③ 몸 움직이기를 좋아해요./몸 움직이기를 싫어해요.

He likes/ doesn't like movements.

④ 내성적이에요./외향적이에요. He is reserved(introvere)/ extrovert.

⑤ 자기 의견을 잘 표현하지 못해요./자기 의견을 잘 표현해요.

He can't/ can express his opinion.

⑥ 매사에 활동적이에요./활동적인 사람이 아니에요.

He is/ is not an active person.

⑦ 진취적이에요./진취적인 사람이 아니에요.

He is adventurous/ not adventurous.

⑧ 적극적이에요./소극적이에요. He is active/ passive.

⑨ 과단성이 있어요./과단성이 없어요. He is decisive/ not decisive.

(2) 집안일보다 외부 일을 중시해요.

He puts more stress on external affairs than family affairs.

① 외부 일보다 집안일을 중시해요.

He puts more stress on family affairs than external affairs.

② 가급적 외부활동을 피하세요./외부활동해도 좋아요.

He avoids/ likes external activities.

③ 예술과 문학을 좋아하고 서정적이에요.

He is a lyrical person who likes art and literature.

④ 예민한 편이에요./무딘 편이에요. He is kind of sensitive/ dull.

⑤ 봉사정신이 많아요./봉사정신이 없어요.

He has lots of/ no service spirit.

⑥ 정의감이 많아요./정의감이 없어요.

He has lots of/ no sense of justice.

⑦ 솔직담백한 성격이에요./비밀이 많아요.

He is forthright/ cryptic.

⑧ 카리스마가 있어요./카리스마가 없어요.

He is/ is not charismatic.

⑨ 독재적인 기질이 있어요./민주적인 기질이 있어요.

He is kind of authoritative/ democratic.

⑩ 과묵해요./말이 많아요./말이 없어요.

He is reserved/ talkative/ quiet.

⑪ 남의 얘기를 잘 듣는 편이에요./남의 얘기를 잘 안 듣는 편이에요.

He is/ isn't a good listener.

⑫ 남의 말을 끝까지 듣는 편이에요.

He tends to hear out others' words.

⑬ 다른 사람이 자신에게 고민거리를 잘 말해요.

He is good at getting it out.

(3) 소심해요./대범해요. He is narrow-minded/ free-hearted.

　① 섬세해요./거칠어요. He is delicate/ rough.

　② 남의 말에 민감한 편이에요./남의 말에 신경 안 쓰는 편이에요.

　　He is sensitive/ indifferent to others.

　③ 경솔한 편이에요./꼼꼼한 편이에요. He is rash/ meticulous.

　④ 성격이 급해요./성격이 느긋해요. He is impatient/ easy-going.

　⑤ 순발력이 좋아요./순발력이 없어요. He has/ lacks quickness.

　⑥ 순간 판단력이 빨라요./순간 판단력이 느려요.

　　He has a quick/ slow sense of judgement.

　⑦ 행동에 거침이 없어요./행동을 조심스럽게 해요.

　　He acts without/ with care.

　⑧ 냉정한 편이에요./관대한 편이에요. He is cool/ generous.

　⑨ 성격이 부드러워요./성격이 거칠어요. He is mild/ tough.

　⑩ 침착해요./흥분을 잘해요. He is calm/ short-tempered.

　⑪ 믿음직해요./믿음이 안 가요. He is reliable/ unreliable.

　⑫ 믿을 수 있는 사람이에요./믿을 수 없는 사람이에요.

　　He is faithful/ unfaithful.

　⑬ 생각에 빈틈이 없어요./생각이 허술해요.

　　He is a man of astuteness./ He is unsophisticated.

　⑭ 창의력이 뛰어나요./창의력이 없어요.

　　He is creative./ He lacks creativeness.

(4) 남과 잘 사귀는 편이에요./사람을 잘 사귀지 못하는 편이에요.

He is sociable./ He is not sociable.

① 남과 잘 싸우는 편이에요./다른 사람과 잘 싸우지 않아요.

He is argumentative./ He is not argumentative.

② 꾸준하게 노력하는 편이에요./자신의 천재성을 믿는 편이에요.

He is hard-working./ He believes in his genius.

③ 인내심이 많아요./인내심이 없어요.

He is patient./ He is impatient.

④ 자신에게 이익이 되는 일에만 적극적이에요.

He is active for only his interest.

⑤ 자신에게 이익이 없어도 적극적으로 일해요.

He is active for what is against his interest.

⑥ 자신에게 불이익이라고 생각하면 일을 하지 않아요.

He doesn't work against his interest.

⑦ 자신에게 불이익이라고 생각해도 일을 해요.

He works hard regardless of his interest.

⑧ 아이디어가 많은 사람이에요./아이디어가 없는 사람이에요.

He has lots of/ no idea.

⑨ 새로운 일에 도전하기 좋아하는 사람이에요./새로운 일에 도전하는 것을 싫어하는 사람이에요.

He enjoys/ hates challenging new tasks.

⑩ 싫증을 잘 느끼는 사람이에요./싫증을 잘 내는 사람이에요./한 번 시작한 일은 끝장을 보는 사람이에요.

He easily gets sick and tired of work./ He is a very patient worker.

⑪ 일단 시작한 일은 반드시 끝을 맺는 사람이에요./계획한 일은 반드시 성취하는 사람이에요.

He is a man of achievement./ He completes whatever he plans.

(5) 예의 바른 사람이에요./예의를 모르는 사람이에요.

He is a very polite person./ He is a rude person.

① 점잖은 사람이에요./점잖지 못한 사람이에요.

He is a decent person./ He is an ill-mannered person.

② 불필요하게 일을 벌이지 않아요./불필요한 일을 벌여요.

He doesn't start unnecessary work./ He starts unnecessary work.

③ 이기적이에요./헌신적이에요. He is selfish./ He is devoted.

④ 소심해요./ 대범해요. He is timid./ He is broad-minded.

⑤ 이기적인 욕심을 드러내요./이기적인 욕심이 있어요./이기적인 욕심이 없어요./여러 사람 앞에서 자기 욕심을 드러내지 못해요./다른 사람 앞에서 자기 욕심을 잘 드러내요.

He shows his selfishness./ He is selfish and greedy./ He is not selfish./ He cannot show his selfishness./ He shows his greediness before others.

⑥ 단기간에 계획된 일은 잘해요./단기간에 계획된 일은 못해요.

He is good at a short-term project./ He is not good at a short-term project.

⑦ 장기적인 일은 잘해요./장기적인 일은 못해요.

He is good at a long-term project./ He is not good at a long-term project.

⑧ 꾸준한 일은 잘해요./일회성 일은 잘해요.

He is good at a steady task./ He is good at a one-time task.

⑨ 아집이 강해요./아집이 없어요.

He has a strong selfishness./ He has no selfishness.

⑩ 의심이 많아요./남을 의심할 줄 몰라요.

He is doubtful./ He never doubts.

⑪ 욕심이 많아요./욕심이 없어요./욕심이 적어요.

He is greedy./ He has no greediness./ He has little greediness.

⑫ 속마음을 잘 내색하지 않아요./속마음이 잘 드러나요.

He doesn't open his heart./ He opens his heart.

⑬ 얼굴색이 잘 변해요./표정관리가 안 돼요./표정 변화가 없어요.

His face changes often./ He cannot manage his face./ He has no change in the face.

⑭ 생각을 많이 해요./생각이 없어요./즉흥적이에요./심사숙고를 잘 해요.

He is very thoughtful./ He is not thoughtful./ He is spontaneous./ He is considerate.

⑮ 추진력이 약해요./추진력이 있어요./추진력이 좋아요./불도저 처럼 밀고 나가요.

He has a weak driving force./ He has a positive drive./ He has a strong driving force./ He is like a bulldozer.

(6) 자신의 일에 소홀해요./자신의 일에 철저해요.

He is negligent of his own affairs./ He is throughgoing for his affair.

① 바깥일을 더 좋아해서 집안 일에 소홀해요.

He likes outside affairs so much that he is negligent of home affairs.

② 남의 일에 참견을 잘해요./남의 일에 무관심해요./남의 일에 관심이 없어요./남의 일에 관심이 많아요.

He is good at cutting in./ He is indifferent to others' affairs./ He is not interested in others' affairs./ He is indifferent to other's work.

③ 자신의 잘못을 잘 몰라요./자신의 잘못을 후회하지 않아요./ 자신의 잘못을 반성하고 있어요.

He doesn't know what is wrong with him./ He has no regrets about his wrongdoing./ He is repenting his past mistake.

④ 자신의 의견을 잘 말하지 않는 편이에요./자신의 주장이 확실해요.

He doesn't give his opinion./ He is extremely self-assertive.

⑤ 조그만 일에도 예민해요./조그만 일에는 대범해요.

He is sensitive to trifle things./ He is broad-minded in trifle things.

⑥ 상대방의 입장을 먼저 생각해요./상대방에 대한 배려가 없어요./상대방에 대한 배려가 부족해요./상대방을 잘 배려해요.

He considers other's position first./ He has no consideration for others./ He is lacking considerations for others./ He is very considerate.

⑦ 일을 쉽게 결정해요./결정력이 약해요.

He makes his decision with ease./ He lacks decisiveness.

⑧ 후회하는 일이 많아요./지나간 일은 후회하지 않아요.

He has many regrets about the past./ He has no regret about

the things past.

⑨ 금방 잊어버려요./잘 잊지 못해요./잊으려고 노력해요./기억하려고 노력해요. He has a short memory./ He is not good at forgetting things./ He tries to forget things./ He tries to remember things.

⑩ 화를 잘 내요./화를 잘 안 내요.

He often gets angry./ He seldom gets angry.

⑪ 일이 마음먹은 대로 안 되면 화가 나요.

He gets angry when things are not done as he wished.

⑫ 후회할 때가 많지만 금방 잊어버려요.

He regrets about things very often, but forgets them soon.

(7) 듬직해요./듬직한 맛이 없어요.

He is reliable./ He is not reliable.

① 말수가 적어요./말이 많아요.

He is a reserved person./ He is talkative.

② 말을 더듬어요./청산유수예요./말을 잘 해요/말을 못 해요.

He stammers./ He is a fluent speaker./ He is eloquent./ He is not a good speaker.

③ 말이 많지는 않지만, 친한 사이끼리는 말을 많이 하는 편이에요.

He is not such a big mouth, but becomes talkative between friends.

④ 말이 과격해요./말이 부드러워요./말이 거칠어요.

He is a violent speaker./ He is a mild speaker./ He is a tough speaker.

⑤ 누구한테건 거리낌 없이 과격한 말을 해요.

He never hesitates to speak radically to others.

⑥ 게으른 편이에요./게으르지 않아요.

He tends to be lazy./ He is not lazy.

⑦ 부지런한 편이에요./부지런해요.

He tends to be diligent./ He is diligent.

⑧ 승부에 강해요./승부에 약해요.

He is strong in competition./ He is not good at competition.

⑨ 승부욕이 많아요./승부욕이 없어요.

He is very competitive./ He has no competitive desire.

⑩ 질투심이 많아요./질투심이 없어요.

He is very jealous./ He has no jealousy.

⑪ 한번 감정이 상하면 오래 가요.

His emotional hurt stays long.

⑫ 마음의 상처를 쉽게 잊지 못해요.

He is not good at getting over emotional hurt.

⑬ 조그만 일은 무시해버려요./조그만 일에 연연해요.

He ignores trifle things./ He is very sensitive to trifle things.

⑭ 세심해요./세심하지 못해요./세심한 면이 부족해요.

He is very prudent./ He is not prudent./ He lacks prudence.

⑮ 치밀해요./치밀하지 못해요./치밀한 면이 부족해요.

He is very well-organized./ He is poorly organized./ He lacks
accuracy.

20

한국 음식
Korean Food

1. 한국 음식 용어 Key Words for Korean Food

1) 한식 *Hanshik* (Korean Dishes)

한식은 한국 고유의 음식이다.

Hanshik(Korean Dishes) is Korean traditional food.

2) 한정식 *Hanjeongshik* (Korean Table d'hote)

한정식은 음식의 종류와 가짓수를 미리 정해 놓은 한국식의 식사를
말한다.

Hanjeongshik(Korean Table d'hote) is formal Korean Meal whose kinds
and numbers are arranged beforehand.

3) 비빔밥 *Bibimbab* (Mixed Rice)

비빔밥은 쌀밥에 고기, 나물, 양념, 장 등을 얹어 비벼먹도록 한 음

식이다.

Bibimbab (Mixed Rice) is a meal of rice mixed with meat, vegetables, condiments, and soy sauce.

4) 전주 비빔밥 *Jeonju Bibimbab* (Mixed Rice Made in Jeonju)

전주 비빔밥은 대한민국 전라북도 전주시의 전통적인 비빔밥을 일컫는다.

전주 비빔밥은 밥에 뜸을 들일 때 콩나물을 넣어 그 김으로 콩나물을 데쳐서 밥과 뒤섞은 다음에 육회, 김, 묵, 쑥갓, 은행, 나물 등을 곁들여 비빈다.

Jeonju Bibimbab is a traditional mixed rice of Jeonju in Jollabuk-do, Korea. While the rice is being boiled, we put bean sprouts, and after the rice is cooked, we put raw beef, seaweed, jelly, some crown daisys, gingco nuts, and wild vegetables to make a bowl of Jeonju mixed rice.

5) 돌솥 비빔밥 *Dolsot Bibimbab* (Mixed Rice Cooked in a Stone Pot)

돌솥 비빔밥은 보통 비빔밥과 같은 식재료를 사용하지만, 비빔밥을 돌로 만든 솥에 넣기 때문에 솥 바닥에 누룽지가 만들어져 색다른 맛을 낸다.

Dolsot Bibimbab(Mixed rice cooked in a stone pot) has the same ingredients, but it is cooked in a stone pot, leaving scorched rice at the bottom, which is called *Nurungji* with a specific flavor.

6) 삼계탕 *Samgyetang* (Chicken Broth with Ginseng and Other Herbs)

삼계탕은 닭 한 마리를 통째로 삶은 음식이다. 이때 닭 속에 인삼,

대추, 마늘 등의 식재료를 함께 넣어 끓인다. 한국에서는 삼계탕을 주로 무더운 여름철에 건강을 지키기 위해 먹는다.

The main ingredient of *Samgyetang*(Chicken broth with ginseng) is a whole chicken boiled in water. Beside the chicken, such ingredients as ginseng, jujube, and garlic are boiled together. In Korea people eat *Samgyetang* to defeat the heat of hot summer.

7) 냉면 *Naengmyeon* (Cold Noodles)

냉면은 메밀가루로 만든 국수에 쇠고기나 돼지고기, 닭고기, 김치, 달걀, 배, 파, 마늘, 생강, 소금, 간장, 기름, 깨소금, 후춧가루, 겨자, 식초, 실고추를 얹어 맛을 낸다.

Naengmyeon(cold noodles) is a bowl of buckwheat flour noodles cooked and seasoned with beef, pork, chicken, kimchi, eggs, a pear, a green onion, garlic, ginger, salt, soy sauce, oil, sesame and salt, pepper, mustard, vinegar, and threaded hot pepper.

냉면에는 국물이 있는 물냉면, 열무김치를 얹은 열무김치냉면, 갖은 식재료를 넣어 국수와 함께 비벼 먹는 비빔냉면 등이 있다.

The types of *Naengmyeon* are water *Naengmyeon*, Young radish *Naengmyeon*, seasoned with young radish *kimchi*, and *Bibim Naengmyeon*, a bowl of cold noodles mixed with diverse ingredients including hot pepper paste.

8) 회 *Hoe* (Raw Fish/ Meat)

회는 날로 먹는 음식을 일컫는다. 일반적으로 회는 생선이나 고기를 썰어서 날로 먹거나 아니면 살짝 데쳐서 초고추장 또는 겨자즙, 초간장에 찍어 먹는다.

Hoe (Raw Fish/ Meat)is a kind of uncooked food. People dip raw fish or minced raw beef in vinegared hot pepper paste, mustard sauce or vinegared soy sauce to eat them.

9) 떡볶이 *Teokbokki* (Hot Rice Cake Stew)

떡볶이는 쌀가루로 만든 떡에 고기, 고추장, 설탕을 넣어 같이 볶은 음식이다.

Teokbokki (Hot Rice Cake Stew)is a broiled dish of sliced rice cake, meat, hot pepper paste, and sugar.

10) 갈비 *Galbi* (Ribs)

갈비는 소나 돼지의 등뼈 부분의 살, 또는 등뼈로 만든 요리이다. 등뼈 부분은 지방이 적고 단백질이 많은 근육으로 이루어져 있어 사람의 뼈에도 도움을 주는 음식이다.

Galbi (Ribs) is a dish made of the flesh on the ribs of a cow or a pig. The flesh on the backbone or ribs, composed of muscles containing much protein and little fat, is also helpful for human bones.

11) 부침개/전 *Buchimgae/ Jeon* (A Flat Cake)

부침개는 '부치개'라고도 하고 '지짐이' 또는 '전'이라고도 한다.

The *Buchimgae* (A Flat Cake) is a fried food made of flat flour dough, which is also called "*Buchigae*", "*Jijimee*" or "*Jeon*".

부침개는 야채나 해물 등의 식재료에 밀가루, 계란 등을 섞어 반죽한 다음에 프라이팬에 기름을 두른 후 부쳐서 먹는 음식이다.

It is a flat flour dough mixed with eggs, vegetables and sea food, which is fried on the oiled pan.

12) 불고기 *Bulgogi* (Broiled Beef)

불고기는 소고기에 여러 가지 양념과 야채를 넣어 자작하게 재웠다가 볶은 음식이다. 돼지고기로 만든 불고기는 소고기로 만든 '불고기'와 구별하기 위해 '돼지 불고기'라 부른다.

Bulgogi(Broiled Beef) is a dish of broiled beef seasoned with vegetables and diverse seasonings. There is also "pork Bulgogi", whose main ingredient is not beef but pork.

13) 된장찌개 *Doenjang Jjigae* (Soybean Paste Pot Stew)

된장찌개는 끓는 육수에 된장을 풀고 육류나 어패류, 채소, 두부, 버섯을 비롯한 각종 식재료를 넣어 함께 끓인 음식이다.

Doenjang Jjigae(Soybeen Paste Pot stew) is a soybean pot stew cooked with meat or seafood, vegetables, bean curd, and mushroom.

14) 김치찌개 *Kimchi Jjigae* (Kimchi Pot Stew)

김치찌개는 김치, 돼지고기, 마늘을 넣고 얼큰하게 끓인 음식이다.
Kimchi Jjigae is a spicy pot stew cooked with *Kimch*, pork and garlic.
김치찌개는 식재료가 간단하고 만들기 쉽기 때문에 한국의 가정에서 흔히 볼 수 있는 음식이다.

It is one of the popular foods in Korean homes owing to the simple recipe.

15) 잡채 *Japchae* (Chop Suey)

잡채는 여러 가지 채소, 소고기, 당면 등의 식재료를 볶아 참기름으로 다시 버무린 후 계란, 참깨 등의 고명을 얹은 음식이다.

Japchae(Chop Suey) is a mixed dish of fried vegetables, meat and Chinese noodles seasoned with eggs and sesame.

16) 신선로 *Shinsollo* (Brass Chafing Dish)

신선로는 왕이나 귀족들만 먹던 한국의 궁중 음식이다.

Shinsollo(Brass Chafing Dish) is a Korean court dish enjoyed by a king or the aristocracy.

신선로는 그릇의 가운데 부분에 숯을 넣도록 되어 있는데 그릇의 가장자리에 고기, 해산물, 채소 등을 넣은 후 국물을 부어 즉석에서 끓여먹게 만든 음식이다.

In the middle of *Shinsollo*, there is charcoal fire, around which meat, sea foods and vegetables are boiled with broth in a chafing-dish.

신선로는 다양한 재료가 필요하고 시간이 정성이 많이 들어가는 고급스럽고 화려한 음식이다.

It is a luxurious and splendid dish requiring diverse materials, time and devotion of the cook.

17) 육개장 *Yukgaejang* (Hot Shredded Beef Soup)

육개장은 소고기, 여러 가지 채소, 고사리, 숙주나물 등을 푹 삶아 끓인 후 고춧가루를 넣어 매운 맛이 나게 만든 음식이다.

Yukgaejang(Hot Shredded Beep Soup) is a hot soup made of long-boiled shredded beef, diverse vegetables, including bracken and green-bean sprout and hot pepper.

18) 낙지볶음 *Nagjibokeum* (Hot Pan-Broiled Octopus)
pan-broiled octopus (seasoned with red pepper)

낙지볶음은 낙지에 양파, 실파, 풋고추, 고추장, 고춧가루, 설탕, 참기름, 파, 마늘, 생강 등을 넣고 같이 볶은 음식이다.

Nagjibokeum(Hot Pan-Broile Octopus) is a pan-broiled dish with octopus, onions, small green onions, green pepper, hot pepper paste or powder, sugar, sesame oil, green onions, garlic, and ginger.

19) 김밥 *Gimbab* (Dried Laver and Rice)

김밥은 밥을 소금과 참기름으로 맛을 내어 김 위에 펼쳐 놓고 시금치, 단무지, 당근, 달걀 등을 길게 놓은 후 말아서 한입 크기로 썰어 낸 음식이다.

Gimbab (Dried laver and rice) is boiled rice seasoned with salt and sesame oil, combined with spinach, pickled radish, and fried eggs and then wrapped with a piece of dried laver. It is usually cut into the size of one bite.

20) 국수 *Guksu* (Noodles)

국수는 쌀가루나 밀가루 등을 반죽하여 길고 가늘게 뽑아 만든 음식이다.

Guksu (Noodles) is the noodles made of rice or flour.

21) 칼국수 *Kalguksu* (Knife Noodles)

칼국수는 육수나 멸치 국물에 반죽된 밀가루를 칼로 잘라서 넣은 후 닭고기, 감자, 호박, 김, 파 등을 넣어 함께 끓인 음식이다.

Kalguksu (Knife Noodles) is a boiled dish made of the noodles cut out with a kitchen knife, chicken, pumpkin, laver and green onions.

22) 우동 *Udong* (Japanese Noodles)

우동은 다시마 국물에 면, 파, 간장, 설탕을 넣고 끓인 음식이다.

Udong (Japanese Noodles) is a dish of Japanese noodles boiled in the kelp soup with green onions, soy sauce and sugar.

23) 카레밥 *Karebab* (Curry and Rice)

카레밥은 고기, 야채, 카레를 섞어 볶은 것을 밥 위에 얹어 내는 음식이다.

Karebab (Curry and Rice) is a dish of boiled rice topped with fried curry, meat, and vegetables.

24) 짜장면 *Jajangmyeon* (Chinese Black Noodles)

짜장면은 야채, 고기, 식용유와 함께 춘장을 넣어 볶은 양념을 국수에 비벼먹는 음식이다.

Jajangmyeon (Chinese Black Noodles) is a dish of noodles combined with fried blackish bean sauce, vegetables, and meat.

25) 짬뽕 *Jjampong* (Chinese Hotchpotch Noodles)

짬뽕은 해산물, 고기, 야채를 기름에 볶은 후 닭이나 돼지뼈로 만든 육수를 넣어 끓인 물에 삶은 국수를 넣어 먹는 음식이다.

Jjampong (Chinese Hotchpotch Noodles) is a Chinese-style hotchpotch noodles boiled in the hot broth of chicken bones or pig bones with fried seafood, meat and vegetables.

26) 울면 *Woolmyeon*

울면은 버섯, 당근 등의 채소와 새우, 오징어, 해삼 등의 해산물, 달걀 등을 부재료로 쓰고 옥수수 녹말로 걸쭉하게 만든 국물에 국수를 말아 먹는 음식이다.

Woolmyeon is a dish of noodles boiled in thick corn starch soup with the ingredients of mushrooms, carrots, shrimps, squids, trepangs and eggs.

27) 탕수육 *Tangsuyuk* (Sweet and Sour Fried Pork/Beef)

탕수육은 돼지고기를 튀겨 식초, 간장, 설탕, 야채, 녹말물 등을 넣고 끓인 소스에 찍어 먹는 음식이다.

Tangsuyuk (Sweet and Sour Fried Pork/ Beef) is deep-fried pork [beef] covered with sweet and sour starchy sauce made of vinegar, soy sauce, sugar, vegetables and starchy water.

28) 라면 *Ramyeon*

라면은 기름에 튀겨서 말린 국수에 스프를 넣어 간단하게 끓여 먹을 수 있도록 만든 즉석 식품이다.

Ramyeon is an instant food composed of dry fried-noodles and powdered soup, which can be eaten after being boiled in water for some minutes.

29) 볶음밥 *Boggeumbab* (Fried Rice)

볶음밥은 밥에 채소와 육류를 넣어 볶아 먹는 음식이다.

Boggeumbab (Fried Rice) is a dish of fried rice mixed with vegetables and meat.

30) 덮밥 *Deopbab* (Covered Rice)

덮밥은 밥 위에 양념을 얹은 음식이다.

덮밥에는 두부 덮밥, 참치 덮밥, 오징어 덮밥, 짜장 덮밥, 달걀 덮밥, 쇠고기 덮밥 등이 있다.

Deopbab (Covered Rice) is a dish of rice covered with specific seasonings or sauces, among which are bean cud and rice, tuna and rice, squid and rice, black bean paste and rice, eggs and rice, beef and rice, etc.

2. 반찬 Side Dishes

1) 김치 *Kimchi*

김치는 무, 배추, 오이 등의 채소를 소금에 절였다가 고추, 파, 마늘, 젓 등의 양념으로 버무려 발효시킨 음식이다.

Kimchi is a fermented food made of salted vegetables such as radish, cabbage, and cucumber mixed with hot pepper, green onions, garlic and pickles.

2) 깍두기 *Kagdugi* (Pickled Radish)

깍두기는 무, 오이 등의 야채를 정방형으로 썰어 여러 가지 양념을 버무려 삭힌 음식이다.

Kagdugi (Picked Radish) is a fermented food made of cubically cut vegetables such as radish and cucumbers mixed with diverse hot seasonings.

3) 생채 *Saengchae* (Chopped Radish)

생채는 계절에 따라 생산되는 싱싱한 채소를 익히지 않고, 초장, 고추장, 겨자장, 설탕, 식초 등으로 무친 음식이다.

Sangchae (Chopped Radish) is made of fresh vegetables seasoned with vinegar-mixed hot pepper paste, hot paper paste, mustard and soy sauce, sugar and vinegar.

4) 오이소박이 *Oisobagi* (Cucumber Kimch)

오이소박이는 오이 속에 여러 가지 양념을 넣어 절여 놓은 음식이다.

Oisobagi (Cucumber Kimch) is pickled cucumber seasoned with diverse seasonings.

5) 나물 *Namul* (Greens/ Wild Vegetables)

나물은 무, 시금치, 미나리, 쑥갓, 오이, 호박, 연근, 고구마, 감자, 가지, 고추, 깻잎, 콩나물, 고사리, 도라지, 쑥, 버섯 등을 볶거나 삶아서 여러 가지 양념을 버무려 놓은 음식이다.

Namul (Greens/ Wild Vegetables) is diverse vegetables mixed with diverse seasonings after being washed, boiled, and fried. They are radish, spinach, dropwort, wild daisy, cucumber, pumpkin, lotus roots, sweet potatoes, potatoes, pepper, sesame leaves, bean sprouts, bracken, wormwood, mushroom, etc.

6) 구이 *Guee* (Grilled Meat)

구이는 돼지고기, 소고기 등을 양념장에 재웠다가 구운 음식이다.

Guee (Grilled Meat) is the dish of pork or beef grilled after being matured in the seasoned soy sauce.

7) 볶음 *Boggeum* (Pan-broiled Dishes)

볶음은 식재료를 양념과 함께 뜨거운 불에 볶아낸 음식이다.

Boggeum (Pan-broiled Dishes) is pan-broiled food cooked with seasonings.

8) 조림 *Jorim* (Boiled Dishes)

조림은 육류나 어패류를 간장이나 고추장에 넣고 끓여 물기가 없도록 조린 음식이다.

Jorim (Boiled Dishes) is the meat or sea food boiled long in soy sauce or hot pepper paste until most of the water got evaporated.

9) 찜 *Jjim* (Steamed Dishes)

찜은 육류, 어패류, 채소 등에 여러 가지 양념을 하여 약간의 물과 함께 끓이거나 수증기로 쪄낸 음식이다.

Jjim (Steamed Dishes) is steamed food using meats, seafoods and vegetables with diverse seasonings.

10) 무침 *Muchim* (Mixed Food)

무침은 조개, 북어, 오징어, 굴 등에 여러 가지 양념을 섞은 음식이다.

Muchim (Mixed Food) is a mixture of specific materials such as shells, a dried walleye pollock, squid and oyster and diverse seasonings.

11) 쌈 *Ssam* (Vegetable Wraps)

쌈은 밥이나 고기 등을 채소에 얹어 싸 먹도록 만든 음식이다.

Ssam (Vegetables Wraps) is wrapping rice or meat in a vegetable.

12) 묵 *Muk* (Jelly)

묵은 메밀, 녹두, 도토리 등을 풀처럼 쑤어 식혀서 굳힌 음식이다.

Muk(Jelly) is a jelly made of glue-type buckwheat, mung-bean and acorn

13) 젓/젓갈 *Jeot/Jeotgal* (Pickles) : 젓갈은 '젓'이라고도 한다.

젓갈은 멸치, 새우, 연어, 조개, 게, 조기, 명란, 창난 등 어패류의 살이나 알, 창자 등을 소금에 절여 발효시킨 음식이다.

Jeotgal(Pickles) is pickled forms of the flesh or eggs of anchovy, shrimp, salmon, shell, crab, croaker, and pollock.

14) 튀김 *Tuigim* (Fries)

튀김은 닭고기나 감자, 김, 오징어 등에 달걀, 밀가루, 녹말가루, 소금, 물을 섞어 튀김옷을 만든 후 뜨거운 기름에 튀겨낸 음식이다.

Tuigim (Fries) is deep fried chicken, potato, or squid in a frying coat made of eggs, flour, starch flour, salt and water

15) 샐러드 Salad

샐러드는 야채, 과일을 주재료로 하여 마요네즈에 버무린 음식이다.

Salad is a mixture of vegetables, fruits, and diverse dressings.

16) 강정 *Gangjeong* (Fried Glutinous Rice Cake)

강정은 닭이나 참깨, 들깨, 콩 등을 볶아 물엿에 버무려 굳힌 것을 말한다.

강정에는 닭강정, 콩강정, 깨강정, 호두강정 등이 있다.

Gangjeong(Fried Glutinous Rice Cake) is fried glutinous materials like chicken, sesame, wild sesame, beans, among which are Chiken Gangjeong, Bean Gangjeong, Sesame Gangjeong, and Walnut Gangjeong.

17) 말이 *Maree* (Rolls)

말이는 계란, 양배추 등의 식재료를 먹기 좋게 돌돌 말아 놓은 음식이다.

Maree(Rolls) is a rolled form for foods such as eggs and lettuce.

18) 전 *Jeon* (Flat Flour Dough)

전은 식재료를 얇게 썰어 밀가루와 달걀을 묻혀 기름에 지진 음식이다.

Jeon (Flat Flour Dough) is a thin fried food on the oiled pan after being coated with flour and eggs.

19) 떡 *Teok* (Rice Cake)

떡은 곡식 가루를 찌거나 익혀서 일정한 형태로 만든 음식이다.

Teok (Rice Cake) is made of powdered grains in a steamed form with diverse patterns or shapes.

20) 장아찌 *Jangajji* (Pickles)

장아찌는 채소에 소금이나 장을 배게 하여 짭짤하게 절인 음식이다.

Jangajji (Pickles) is vegetable food pickled salty in soy sauce or salt.

3. 조미료 Seasonings

1) 간장 *Ganjang* (Soy Sauce)

2) 식초 *Shikcho* (Vinegar)

3) 참기름 *Chamgirum* (Sesame Oil)

4) 고추장 *Gochujang* (Hot Pepper Paste)

5) 참깨 *Chamggae* (Sesame)

6) 소금 *Sogeum* (Salt)

7) 후추 *Hoochoo* (Pepper)

8) 설탕 *Seoltang* (Sugar)

9) 꿀 *Ggul* (Honey)

10) 버터 Butter

4. 야채류 Vegetables

1) 도라지 *Doraji* (Wormwood)

2) 당근 *Danggeun* (Carrot)

3) 연근 *Yeongeun* (Lotus Root)

4) 버섯 *Beoseot* (Mushroom)

5) 배추 *Baechoo* (Cabbage)

6) 오이 *Oyee* (Cucumber)

7) 상추 *Sangchoo* (Lettuce)

8) 파 *Pa* (Green Onion)

9) 양파 *Yangpa* (Onion)

10) 마늘 *Maneul* (Garlic)

11) 시금치 *Shigeumchi* (Spinach)

12) 토마토 *Tomato*

5. 과일 Fruits

1) 잣 *Jot* (Pine Nut)

2) 밤 *Bam* (Chestnut)

3) 호두 *Hodoo* (Walnut)

4) 은행 *Eunhaeng* (Gingko Nut)

5) 사과 *Sagwa* (Apple)

6) 배 *Bae* (Pear)

7) 귤 *Gyul* (Tangerine)

8) 복숭아 *Boksungah* (Peach)

9) 수박 *Soobok* (Watermelon)

10) 딸기 *Ddalgi* (Strawberry)

11) 바나나 Banana

12) 파인애플 Pineapple

13) 포도 *Podo* (Grapes)

14) 감 *Gam* (Persimmon)

6. 곡식 Grains

1) 콩 *Kong* (Bean)

2) 찹쌀 *Chapssal* (Glutinous Rice)

3) 보리 *Bori* (Barley)

4) 쌀 *Ssal* (Rice)

5) 팥 *Pot* (Red bean)

6) 고구마 *Goguma* (Sweet Potato)

7) 감자 *Gamja* (Potato)

7. 음료 Beverage

1) 우유 *Wooyoo* (Milk)

2) 맥주 *Maekju* (Beer)

3) 생맥주 *Saeng Maekju* (Draft Beer)

4) 커피 Coffee

5) 녹차 *Nokcha* (Green Tea)

6) 홍차 *Hongcha* (Black Tea)

7) 인삼차 *Insamcha* (Ginseng Tea)

8) 유자차 *Youjacha* (Citron Tea)

9) 매실차 *Maeshilcha* (Plum Tea)

10) 오미자차 *Omijacha* (Maximowiczia Typica)

8. 생선 Fish

1) 장어 *Janguh* (Eel)

2) 명태 *Myeongtae* (Wall Eye Pollock)

3) 조기 *Jogi* (Croaker)

4) 새우 *Saewoo* (Shrimp)

5) 조개류 *Jogae* (Shells)

6) 굴 *Gul* (Oyster)

7) 전복 *Jeonbok* (Ear Shell)

8) 오징어 *Ojinguh* (Squid)

9) 게 *Ge* (Crab)

10) 해삼 *Haesam* (Trepang)

9. 고기 Meat

1) 닭고기 *Dark Gogi* (Chicken)

2) 개고기 *Gae Gogi* (Dog Meat)

3) 소고기 *So Gogi* (Beef)

4) 돼지고기 *Dwaeji Gogi* (Pork)

5) 오리고기 *Ori Gogi* (Duck Meat)

6) 양고기 *Yang Gogi* (Mutton)

10. 기타 Others

1) 담배 *Dambae* (Cigaret)

2) 빙과류 *Binggwaryu* (Ices)

3) 인삼 *Insam* (Ginseng)

4) 땅콩 *Ddangkong* (Peanut)

5) 밀가루 음식 *Milgaroo Eumshik* (Flour food)

6) 매운 음식 *Maewoon Eumshik* (Hot and Spicy Food)

7) 짠 음식 *Jjan Eumshik* (Salty Food)

8) 맵고 짠 음식 *Mapgo Jjan Eumshik* (Hot and Salty Food)

9) 따뜻한 음식 *Ddaddeuthan Eumshik* (Warm Food)

10) 찬 음식 *Chan Eumshik* (Cold Food)

11) 딱딱한 음식 *Ddakddakhan Eumshik* (Hard Food)

12) 부드러운 음식 *Budeureowoon Eumshik* (Soft Food)

13) 지방이 많은 음식 *Jibangee Maneun Eumshik* (Food with much fat)

14) 지방이 적은 음식 *Jibangee Joegeun Eumshik* (Food with little fat)

15) 담백한 음식 *Dambaekhan Eumshik* (Simple and dry food)

16) 싱거운 음식 *Shinggeowoon Eumshik* (Flat Food)

11. 유용한 표현 Useful Expressions

1) 뜨거운 음식을 좋아해요./찬 음식을 좋아해요./시원한 음식을 좋
아해요. I like hot food/ cold food/ cool food.

뜨거운 음식을 싫어해요./찬 음식을 싫어해요./시원한 음식을 싫
어해요. I hate hot food/ cold food/ cool food.

2) 비린 음식을 좋아해요./비린 음식을 싫어해요. I like fishy food./ I
hate fishy food.

생선을 좋아해요./생선을 싫어해요. I like fish./ I hate fish.

3) 채소를 좋아해요/채소를 싫어해요. I like vegetables./ I hate vegetables.

4) 육식을 좋아해요./육식을 싫어해요. I like meat./ I hate meat.

채식을 좋아해요./채식을 싫어해요. I like vegetarian food./ I hate
vegetarian food.

고기 없으면 밥을 못 먹어요. I can't eat without meat.

5) 채식주의자예요./채식주의자 아니에요. I'm a vegetarian./ I'm not
a vegetarian.

찾아보기 Appendix

A

B

C

저자 소개

장미영
현재 전주대학교 교양학부 교수
문학 박사
세계비교문학회 이사
한국문학이론과비평학회 편집위원
전북대학교병원 문예치료 전담강사
한국여성연구소 편집위원
전북대학교 국어국문학과 학사, 석사, 박사 졸업

주요 논저
『21세기 대중 취향과 미디어』, 수필과비평사
『다문화사회 바로서기』, 글솟대
『속해 독서법』, 글누림
『언어와 대중매체』, 신아출판사
『스토리텔링의 이해』, 글누림 외 다수.

김철수
현재 전주대학교 교양학부 교수
문학 박사/시인
한국 제임스 조이스 학회 총무이사
기독교세계관 학술 동역회 전주지부장
조선대학교 영어영문학과 학사, 석사, 박사 졸업
영국 University of Warwick, English and Comparative Literature 석사

주요 논저
"레미제라블에 나타난 은혜와 율법", 기독교학문연구회, 2013.
"Bob Doran's Fall : From the Viewpoint of Eastern Philosophy", James Joyce Society Korea, 2012.
"올리버 트위스트 : 맹자의 성선설로 다시 읽어보기", 한국동서비교문학회, 2012.
"신사와 군자 : 『위대한 유산』, 동양철학으로 다시 읽기", 한국비교문학회, 2011.
"The Theme of 'Zhong-shu (忠恕)' in 'A Painful Case'", James Joyce Society Korea, 2010 외 다수.